being zen

being zen

Bringing Meditation to Life

Ezra Bayda

SHAMBHALA
BOSTON & LONDON · 2003

SHAMBHALA PUBLICATIONS, INC.
Horticultural Hall
300 Massachusetts Avenue
Boston, Massachusetts 02115
www.shambhala.com

9 8 7 6 5 4 3 2 1

FIRST PAPERBACK EDITION
Printed in the United States of America

♾ This edition is printed on acid-free paper that meets the
American National Standards Institute z39.48 Standard.
Distributed in the United States by Random House, Inc.,
and in Canada by Random House of Canada Ltd

THE LIBRARY OF CONGRESS CATALOGUES THE
HARDCOVER EDITION OF THIS BOOK AS FOLLOWS:
Bayda, Ezra.
Being zen: bringing meditation to life/Ezra Bayda.
p. cm.
ISBN 1-57062-856-4
ISBN 1-59030-013-0 (PAPERBACK)
1. Zen meditions. I. Title.
BQ9289.5.B39 2002
294.3'927—dc21   2001044166

To the memory of Susan Loda,
who lived the practice life
with courage, kindness, and grace

Contents

Foreword

LIVING IN OUR "ADVANCED" culture, its increasing unease becomes obvious: the faster we race toward our many goals, the less we know of serenity and satisfaction. Life, for most of us, remains a wearying puzzle. Although we may try to be indifferent to our predicament, this evasion is again unsatisfactory.

Until we realize that we are truly nothing but life itself, we will keep trying to change and manipulate life in hopes of solving the terrifying puzzle it presents. We may even stumble toward the real teachings that exist in the great religions and also outside of them. But it is difficult to understand them as more than concepts (which may assist us to a degree but falls short of the mature, integrated understanding we long for). So what do we do?

A big, big question! Many excellent books describe very well the human predicament, its elements and structure. Very few of them are helpful in making clear what is involved in developing a genuinely useful practice. To say "Just let it go" is like telling an exhausted drowning person to "Just swim to shore."

If you want to wake up, not just talk about it, this book will give you practical guidance—the kind of guidance that you need. Not simplistic, formulaic "Just do it this way" guidance, but words that give you practical help, combined with encouragement—even inspiration—for your efforts. And even though all reading is preliminary, it is often a crucial first step. Both for beginning students and for longtime practitioners, this book will clarify the muddy waters.

And Ezra, the guide? Although I have known him for years as a student, a friend, and now a fellow teacher, I hesitate to string a lot of nice adjectives with his name—these are never the exact truth of a person. But I do live with Ezra's kindness, his steadiness and keen perceptiveness—and most of all, his unceasing practice. And I am confident in recommending his book to you. Enjoy it and benefit.

—Charlotte Joko Beck

Acknowledgments

I WISH TO EXPRESS MY DEEP GRATITUDE to Charlotte Joko Beck, my teacher and friend. Much of what I have learned, and much of what appears in this book, comes directly from my work with her. I'd also like to thank Stephen Levine and Pema Chödrön, both of whom have strongly influenced my path, especially helping to temper the precision and discipline of my Zen training with the more heartfelt quality of loving-kindness.

Many thanks to Carolyn Miller, who voluntarily typed the entire text without complaint, making many valuable suggestions along the way. I'm also grateful to my daughter, Jenessa, for her thorough and merciless editing. Just knowing I would be subject to her scrutiny inspired me to be clearer.

When I submitted my manuscript to the publisher, I thought it was complete and ready to go. Little did I know! It was my good fortune to work with Emily Hilburn Sell, who shaped and edited my words, cutting out the deadwood while skillfully highlighting the unifying themes. I am indebted to her for bringing this book into its present form. In the process we became good friends.

I would also like to thank Elizabeth Hamilton, my wife, friend, and teacher—but not just for her invaluable suggestions on the text. I consider her unwavering support, as well as the strength of her own practice, to be instrumental in helping me to learn what I have learned these last years—the learning out of which this book developed.

Introduction

THE READER WILL NOTICE that throughout this book I rarely use Zen or Buddhist terminology, such as *emptiness* or *nonduality*. In language and in content, I have tried to avoid the esoteric and philosophical. This aversion to the philosophical has been a consistent theme in my life; in fact, I left graduate school in philosophy because it was too philosophical!

Besides, the point of spiritual practice can never be reduced to an intellectual theory or formula. Understanding must be rooted in our experience, and our ability to understand practice is always tempered by where we are on the path of spiritual awakening. At many points along the path, we may even find ourselves wondering what practice really is. Although I have practiced Zen meditation for many years, in this book I have tried to expand the definition of "practice" beyond just meditation technique to include any genuine meditation-based approach. It doesn't matter to me whether you sit Zen, vipassana, Tibetan, or whatever. What matters is whether you want practice to include your everyday living.

Mainly we need a clear approach to help us learn from our life experiences. Consequently I have divided this book into three parts, each pertaining to a different aspect of the path to awakening. Part I describes the basics of what is referred to as "practice," including the essential components of meditation. But it does so with the assumption that the reader already has some elemental familiarity with sitting meditation. If that is not the case, it would be best to get basic meditation instruction in person, particularly to learn the specifics on posture and breathing.

Part II emphasizes how practice can and must be an integral part of our emotional life, focusing especially on becoming free of the constriction of fear. As our protective veneer wears thin, we'll find ourselves encountering more and more frightening or painful experiences. Sometimes we can enter into them deeply. Other times we'll resist mightily. Whatever happens, everything we meet is an opportunity to practice. Everything that comes up is an opportunity to learn. This is especially true of our disappointments. To the extent that we can learn from our disappointments, to that extent we will be able to practice with all the ups and downs of life.

Part III is about awakening the heart of compassion, in which we begin to understand and taste the most essential component of the practice life—the willingness to just be. The more this willingness penetrates the very fabric of our life, the more we can step back from the self-judgments and the all-too-serious preoccupation with our own drama. We can learn to be at home, even in the midst of the muddy water of our lives. This book is about learning what it takes to cultivate that willingness. As we open to the willingness to just be, a sense of spaciousness develops around our suffering. It is my wish that this book guide you toward this experience of spaciousness. For isn't this what we all want—to experience the equanimity that arises when we can willingly be with our life as it is?

the basics of practice

I

Skating on Thin Ice

I HAVE A PICTURE ON MY WALL of a girl ice-skating. She's gliding along, arms held high and head thrown back. Seemingly carefree, she's oblivious to a nearby sign: BEWARE OF THIN ICE. Does this sound familiar?

Most of us cruise through life on automatic pilot. Perhaps things are going well, or at least our life is currently disaster-free. We may have a decent job, supportive relationships, and good physical health, yet even as we glide along, we have an intangible sense of how thin the ice beneath us is. We can sense the anxious quiver that vibrates with vague dissatisfaction, fields of unhealed pain, and unaddressed fears. Yet most of the time we choose not to look beneath the surface.

When our life takes a turn for the worse, when we start encountering cracks in the ice, what do we do? We try to clean up the surface, making our usual efforts to push away or overcome the difficulties. Or we might try to skate around the cracks by ignoring or suppressing our reactions to unpleasant events.

In an attempt to keep from falling through the cracks in the ice, we choose our strategy, either working harder at maintaining control of our lives or making misguided attempts to escape from our difficulties with diversions, pleasures, or busyness. Rarely do we question our strategies, which are always rooted in fear. We believe in them as the unquestioned truth. Yet in doing so, we define our own boundaries, our own restrictions. Consequently our life narrows down to a sense of vague dissatisfaction.

What are these strategies that we use to erect a seemingly solid ground in order to avoid facing our fears? They are as varied as people's personalities. Some are strategies of control—trying to maintain order to ward off a sense of impending chaos. Some are strategies of success involving the drive to get ahead, to be on top—geared to override that nagging inner compulsion to prove our worth. There are strategies of conformity that seek the imagined comfort of fitting in, and strategies of nurturing—hoping to find security in being needed and appreciated. There are also strategies of neediness, in which we assume the identity of weakness and desperately attempt to be saved by a person, a group, or an institution; and strategies of diversion—seeking one pleasure after another to fill the deep holes of longing and loneliness. The list goes on and on.

Sometimes we have to fall right into the icy water, unable to move or breathe, overwhelmed and drowning, before we're forced to deal with the deep-seated conditioning that runs our life—all the land mines of anger, fear, and confusion. It might take an illness, a financial upheaval, a relationship failure, or the death of someone close to us to wake us up and force us to just be in that icy water.

When we fall into these unwanted situations, we can no longer strategize to avoid facing our pain. It's right in front of us! The loss of financial security, our health, or a relationship, for example, will bring fear right to the surface, and we're likely to feel anger, self-pity, depression, and confusion. How we work with these will be a measure of how we understand what our life is truly about. The good fortune of having a strong and genuine spiritual practice may enable us to do something besides just seek comfort and escape when we're hit with one of life's inevitable blows.

In the early seventies I bought a house with a little land in northern California. For eleven years we cultivated an extensive organic garden. Our goal was to live from the land, which included raising goats for milk and chickens and sheep for meat. It was a nice life, and we felt satisfaction in being able to raise our children in the healthiest way we knew how. But when my wife and I both came down with severe immune system disorders, high levels of DDT residue were found in our blood. The DDT had been buried on our property prior to our owning it, and the poisons had made their way into our bodies indirectly through the vegetables and meat that we were so carefully raising. The prolonged exposure consequently broke down our immune systems. Ironically the effort to live a healthy organic lifestyle had contributed to the onset of chronic debilitating disease.

There was no one to blame. Burying the leftovers was just what people did to dispose of pesticides in those days. Our strategy to make our world safe and secure had failed. We had been skating on thin ice. No matter what we do, no matter how good our intentions are, there's no way to guarantee that we can avoid falling into the icy water. Try as we will, there's no way we can strategize and control our world so that difficulties won't befall us. The real issue is whether we will learn from the helplessness that arises when our strategies fail. When my life fell apart with the onset of the immune system disease, it took me many years to really understand the great teaching of the helplessness of the loss of control.

But even when we learn from these major upsets, as soon as we get back on our feet, we often go right back to gliding on the thin ice. Perhaps we know a little about the big hole we've just fallen into, but what about the rest of the cracks in the ice? Can we begin to learn from the smaller cracks—our upsets, our mood swings, our efforts to protect, defend, push away—all our disappointments?

What is required is that we see clearly how we keep ourselves skating on thin ice—how we use identities, strategies, and mental pictures to help keep ourselves going. We need to see our forceful determination to make our strategies work. Then when life situations that don't suit us arise, challenging our identities and our sense of comfort, we can open to the possibility of learning two basic lessons.

First, we can learn to recognize that the difficulty is our path instead of trying to escape from it. This is a radical yet necessary change in our perspective. When uncomfortable things happen to us, we rarely want to have anything to do with them. We might respond with the belief "Things shouldn't be this way" or "Life shouldn't be so messy." Who says? Who says life shouldn't be a mess? When life is not fitting our expectations of how it's supposed to be, we usually try to change it to fit our expectations. But the key to practice is not to try to change our life but to change our relationship to our expectations— to learn to see whatever is happening as our path.

Our difficulties are not obstacles to the path; they are the path itself. They are opportunities to awaken. Can we learn what it means to welcome an unwanted situation, with its sense of groundlessness, as a wake-up call? Can we look at it as a signal that there is something here to be learned? Can we allow it to penetrate our hearts? By learning to do this, we are taking the first basic step toward learning what it means to open to life as it is. We are learning what it means to be willing to be with whatever life presents us. Even when we don't like it, we understand that this difficulty is our practice, our path, our life.

Second, when hardship strikes, we can learn not to point the finger of blame—at another person, at ourselves, at an institution, or even at life itself—and instead turn our attention inward. When we're in distress, this is often one of the hardest things to do, because we so want to defend ourselves. We so want to be right. But it is much more helpful to look at what we ourselves have brought to the situation—beliefs, expectations, requirements, and cravings. Then we might gradually come to understand that whenever we're having an emotional reaction, it's a signal that we have some belief system in place that we haven't yet looked at deeply enough. With practice this understanding gradually becomes our basic orientation.

Intellectually we may realize that we need to look deeply inside, yet we don't really know it. There are people we laugh at because they can't see the most obvious things about themselves. Well, those people are us! We have to acknowledge that we often simply don't want to see the aspects of ourselves that cause us distress. We basically want life to please us—to feel comfortable and secure. Our last priority is to expose our own shaky supports, the tenuous beliefs that stand between us and unknown territory. Why? Because investigating ourselves at this level doesn't necessarily feel good. But until we become aware of all the ways in which we keep ourselves oblivious to what lies under the ice, we will continue to simply glide along with no direction.

What we need is a gradual yet fundamental change in our orientation to life—toward a willingness to see, to learn, to just be with whatever we meet. Perhaps there is nothing more basic and essential than this willingness to just be. To simply be with our experience—even with the heaviness and darkness that surround our suffering—engenders a sense of lightness and heart. The willingness to learn from our disappointments and disillusionments is key. Pain we thought we could never endure becomes approachable. As we cultivate our willingness to just be, we discover that everything is workable. Until we come to know what this means, we are cutting ourselves off from the openness, the connectedness, and the appreciation that are our human gifts.

2
Fast, Cheap, and Out of Control

THE MOVIE *Fast, Cheap, and Out of Control* documents the lives of four unusual men. The first is a lion tamer in a circus. The second designs and builds robots, including little robots created to walk on the moon. The third is a scientist who becomes an expert on the private life of a hairless mammal called the mole rat. The fourth is a gardener who has spent fifty years pruning giant bushes into animal shapes.

Although I have called these men unusual, they are actually quite normal. What they share with one another and with all of us is that each in his own way is trying to maintain control in an essentially uncontrollable world. What is unusual about them is their occupations, which amplify what we all do in our own particular way: attempt to control the world in order to provide ourselves the illusion of security and happiness.

The lion tamer's control strategy is never to show fear. Every time he leaves the cage, he is dripping with sweat, but he never lets the lions know that he's afraid. He must maintain the illusion that he is in charge. Even when a lion bites his calf and blood is dripping into his boot, he won't leave the cage. He stays to finish the act, to maintain his stance of control of these animals, knowing they could tear him apart in the blink of an eye.

The robot designer wants to create machines that will do his bidding in order to make the world a more efficient place. Yet he discovers that he can't exactly make the robots walk. All he can do is program a sequence of mechanical actions that might result in walking. This relatively simple task gives him a glimpse into the incredible complexity of human movement and the difficulty of programming change. Yet still he looks for a way to maintain the illusion of control.

The man who researches mole rats sets up elaborate displays in museums that illustrate how, like ants and bees, mole rats have a self-contained and intelligent community. He tries to duplicate the mole rats' natural habitat, which is an elaborate maze of underground tunnels. He realizes that in nature something as ordinary as the foot of a passing elephant could crush and destroy this entire tunnel world. But knowing the arbitrary dangers in the mole rats' natural environment doesn't stop him from doing everything possible to create artificial conditions under which he can ward off any danger and guarantee safety.

The gardener has spent half a century working in a wealthy woman's extensive garden, manually pruning large bushes into incredible animal-shaped topiary. Yet a single storm could destroy years of his work. The movie portrays him walking helplessly through his garden in the midst of an icy rainstorm, an image that evokes the gut feeling of groundlessness that comes when we realize how flimsy our control strategies are. Despite his diligence, he can never control the damage that nature's forces might wreak.

Like these four men, all of us are doing whatever it is we do to shape our world in accordance with our illusion of control. Our world becomes small and insulated as we focus on some little corner of our self-centered dream, trying to bolster our sense of comfort and security. And yet no matter how tight our strategy is, we're all just one doctor's visit away from losing control.

The Tibetan Buddhist teacher Pema Chödrön likens our ego to a room, a protective cocoon we spin exactly as we'd like it. The temperature is always just right, we hear only the music we want to hear, we eat only the food we want to eat, and perhaps best of all, we only allow the people we like into our room. In short, we make our life exactly the way we want it—pleasing, comfortable, and safe.

But when we step outside the room, what happens? We meet the messiness of everyday life, particularly all those irritating people we're trying to shut out of our room and all the difficult and unwanted situations we're trying so hard to avoid. The more we meet this unpleasantness, the more we want to retreat into our room, our protective cocoon. We close the windows and even cover them with bars and shutters. We put special locks on the doors. We do whatever we can to shut life out.

But if we're fortunate, one day we might wake up to the realization that our room is a substitute life. In trying to control our world to make it comfortable and safe, we've narrowed our existence to the point where we're living a substitute life, one built on the foundation of our desire to avoid our deep core fears—fears of helplessness, of being alone, of being unworthy, of experiencing the anxious quiver of being. And the extent to which we wish to avoid these fears is reflected like a mirror in how we experience our life, because they close us down and hold us back. They numb us to our desire to live a genuine life. They block our aspiration to live from our naturally open heart. And consequently, even as we maintain our control strategies, we slowly stagnate in dissatisfaction, frustration, and a sense of disconnectedness. These are the signs that we are living in the self-imposed prison of a substitute life.

When we are lucky enough to wake up to our situation, we gradually understand that it is only through living a practice life that this substitute life can be transformed into a more genuine life. A practice life might include meditation, but it certainly can't be limited to that. It must also include working with all the ways we keep ourselves from living a genuine life: our idealized pictures of how life is supposed to be, our pretenses, our self-images, our blind spots, our protective behavioral strategies, our knee-jerk reactions of anger, fear, and confusion.

There's a Native American proverb that expresses awakening to this heartfelt desire to live an open and genuine life:

Of the many paths that there are in this life,
There is only one that is worthwhile—
The path of the truly human being.

Interestingly one of the essential ingredients of a genuine life is the understanding that everything in our life is the path, that whatever we encounter can be used to help us awaken. In large part our efforts at control are geared toward preventing us from feeling our core pain, our core fears. All our ideals, all our expectations become a demand that life be a particular way. But this demand—this fear-based effort to control our life, this ego drive to build a protective cocoon—has to be seen for what it is. And objective self-knowledge is the way we begin to see where and how we're protecting and defending. This is why it is such an important aspect of the path of awakening.

We awaken to this self-knowledge through the practice of self-observation, whereby we begin to observe ourselves relentlessly, almost as if we were outside ourselves. Unlike our ordinary focus on ourselves, in which we spin repetitively—thinking about ourselves, analyzing ourselves, and identifying with our situation—the "observer's" focus is objective. It is not analytical, nor is it judgmental. It simply sees what we do, how we think, what we think about, how and when we react, what our basic personal strategies are, what our basic identities are, what our core fears are. In observing ourselves objectively in all kinds of situations, we can begin to see clearly the components of our substitute life: fear-based ideas about how we're supposed to be, how others are supposed to be, how life is supposed to be. We can begin to see the requirements we make of life and how we use them to gain the illusion of control.

The observer helps us look objectively at what's happening: what our thoughts are, what specific reaction we're having, what we do with it. This is not introspection; it's just awareness, awareness of our conditioning in all its manifestations. Nor are we looking at our conditioning as history, focusing on why we are the way we are, but simply as part of what is going on. In observing objectively, without our usual tendency to see everything as good or bad, we develop a sense of spaciousness that allows us to observe from a broader vista than our usual narrow identification. We're able to recognize that whenever we're having an emotional reaction, there's something within us—something running us—that we don't quite see. Knowing this and approaching our emotional reactions with curiosity offers us a clue about where and how we are trying to control our world to suit us.

For example, imagine that someone criticizes us publicly. We react immediately with anger. Then we might move directly to self-justification and blaming, locked into a tape loop of thought. As feelings of rage rise to the surface, we might obsess on how unfair this person is or even on how unfair life is. But if something in us remembers the practice life, we will recall that our emotional reaction is an alarm clock to wake us up to what's actually going on. Then the observer will kick in and start noticing the repeating thought "This isn't fair," even as the internal turmoil continues. We might then see that our emotional reaction is arising directly from our requirement that life *should* be fair. As this becomes clear, it may be possible to observe and then experience the layer of fear from which this requirement is born: the fear of being helpless when we lose control. All our lives we've tried to make life fit our pictures so that we wouldn't have to experience core fears like this one.

Where are we lion-taming—trying to create the illusion of control to hold back the tide? Where are we creating inner robots—following mechanical patterns to just live efficiently or securely, unaware of what really makes us tick? Where are we creating protected habitats or pruning bushes into animal shapes—pretending that the elephant's foot or the icy rains will not touch our secure world? To find the answer, we need only look at our emotional upsets, which are always a clue that there's some picture, some identity, that we're still holding too tightly.

We can then ask ourselves the simple practice question "What is going on right now?" Are we just trying to look good? Are we motivated by the need simply to be comfortable or secure? Are we ruled by the desire for money or possessions? Does our distress come from our pursuit of status or power? Does our anxiety tie in to our craving for approval? Are we just holding on, trying to maintain control? All these patterns lead to a life of no real satisfaction—in other words, a substitute life.

When we understand the connection between our emotional distress and our expectations of what life should be, we can enter more deeply into an experiential practice life. Our path will take us directly to our core pain—into the helplessness of the loss of control, our fear of rejection or abandonment, our basic belief of separateness. As we enter into this place that we've avoided for so long, we discover our capacity to just be there without getting lost or overwhelmed. We experience that it's our *willingness to just be* with the difficult place that engenders a spaciousness around it. We learn that we can let this place penetrate our hearts.

Until we turn and face what we've spent our whole lives avoiding, what are we really doing with our lives? Practice is not some pretty thing we do just on a meditation cushion. Until we learn to observe ourselves objectively, we will remain prisoners of our substitute life. Yet as we live the practice life, looking with increasing honesty at all the ways that we've held ourselves back in fear, we can also begin to experience the freedom of stepping outside our protected room and into the genuine life that awaits us.

3

Swiss Cheese

LET'S IMAGINE OURSELVES as a big piece of Swiss cheese, including all the holes. The holes are our identities, mental constructs, desires, blind spots, stuck places—all those aspects of ourselves that seem to get in the way of realizing our "cheese nature." Sometimes when a meditator gets a glimpse that he's the whole cheese, he forgets that he's also the little holes and instead sees himself as a big cheese. However, we are more likely to identify solely with the little holes—being fearful, being a victim, being confused, being right, and so on. In doing so, we forget our basic cheese nature—the vastness, God, call it what you will. We are the little holes; we can't ignore that. But we're also the whole cheese, and we can't ignore that either. When we finally see the little holes for what they are, then we see they are truly holes—that is, of no substantial reality.

As with all analogies, this one falls short of presenting a complete or accurate view of the practice life, but the point of self-observation is to see which little holes we find ourselves believing in. We might then also see how our belief in the substantiality of these little holes prevents us from experiencing the big whole. This understanding is not theoretical; it has to be experiential. How does the practice life take us there?

One common approach to practice is to emphasize breakthrough or "enlightenment" experiences, in which we pierce the bubble of our normal consciousness, seeing clearly and profoundly into what is real. One problem with this approach is that often we mistakenly take these openings for some higher reality, other than the natural order of things. The whole focus of practice then centers on having an experience, assuming that only with this experience will come permanent freedom—enlightenment. This is a very romantic view. It is also a fantasy. No experience is permanent. Nor can any singular experience make us permanently free. This is not to say that these experiences are not useful. They can be inspiring; they can help point the way. But unless our practice filters directly into our everyday life, what's the point?

There is another approach to practice, one that is not nearly as romantic as seeking after enlightenment. It involves practicing directly with what is, whatever it is. I call this living the practice life. It particularly involves coming back again and again to the present moment, which, of course, has always been an essential aspect of Zen and other contemplative traditions. What separates this approach from seeking experiences is the emphasis on working with issues that we would normally not regard as "spiritual." In fact, they're often the issues we wish would go away. They're all the moldy little holes in the Swiss cheese.

Do we walk around in anxiety or confusion? Do we get angry whenever we're criticized? Do we live our life with a deep and pervasive sense of shame? In what activities are we driven by fear? Can we extend kindness toward ourselves? Is there even one person we can't forgive? In practicing with these sticky questions—in allowing the messiness of our everyday lives to clarify them *experientially*—the bigger picture naturally becomes clearer.

For example, when anger arises in our everyday life circumstances, we can let anger be our practice. As much as we would prefer to be calm, peaceful, and clear, the reality of the present moment is anger. Until we attend to that anger from a practice perspective, it will continue to narrow our life and close our heart. On the other hand, working directly with the anger cultivates our ability to open to the willingness to just be.

How do we work directly with anger—or for that matter with any strong emotion? How can we work with all the holes in our "cheese nature"? In working with my teacher, Joko Beck, I have learned two particular approaches. The first involves clarifying our belief systems, and the second is experiencing the physical reality of the present moment. Clarifying our belief systems is simply modern terminology for the ancient and universal teaching "Know thyself." It involves precise self-observation—seeing how we think, what we think, how we react, what our personal strategies are. As we practice observing ourselves, we gradually become intimately familiar with our particular system, including all the beliefs and attitudes that run our life.

Clarifying our beliefs is not about analyzing or eradicating or changing them. It's about seeing clearly what they are (not what they're about).

The primary tool that we use to clarify our beliefs is *thought-labeling*. In many meditation practices, the instruction is: When thoughts arise, let them go. The instruction is to try to calm and clear the mind. This is nice if we can do it, but often we can't simply let thoughts go. Our minds can be very busy and stay that way for long periods of time. It seems that we humans cannot so easily bypass our evolutionary inheritance of an overactive brain. In some meditation practices, the instruction for dealing with these ever-rising thoughts is to say, "Thinking"—thereby breaking the identification with the thinking—and then return the attention to the breath or some other focus point. Although this is a definite improvement on just trying to let thoughts go, it still doesn't really help clarify what we're up to. This is where thought-labeling comes in.

Thought-labeling is a precise tool that can help in two ways. First, it breaks our identification with our thinking, allowing us to learn to see our thoughts as just thoughts. Second, it allows us to know *what* we're thinking. Let's say you're sitting in meditation, trying to be aware of the breath, and you notice that you're thinking about what a busy day you have ahead of you. To thought-label, you would simply repeat this thought to yourself, saying, "Having a thought that I have too much to do." It's like having a parrot on your shoulder, stating the thoughts verbatim as they arise in the mind.

At first thought-labeling may seem very mental. It may seem as if the labeling itself were making our minds spin more than ever. But that's only because we're not used to it. It takes time for thought-labeling to break us out of our mental tape loops. Just to get some experience with the process, we might start by spending at least five minutes near the beginning of each meditation period labeling every thought. After that we don't need to label all the thoughts. For example, when I find myself thinking inconsequential or mundane thoughts, I use generic labels such as "planning," "fantasizing," "daydreaming," or "conversing." Labeling this way makes it clear to me what my mind is doing. And it usually interrupts the pattern enough to move me out of the mental realm.

However, when I become aware of even the hint of an emotion, I return to labeling the specific thought. For example, I'm meditating and my body is starting to ache from sitting still in a cross-legged position. I become aware that I'm feeling agitated and catch my mind believing that this is too hard. I immediately identify the thought, saying to myself, "Having a believed thought that this is too hard." "Having a believed thought that I have to move." After some practice labeling in this way, the unspoken thought that's running the whole show—if there is one—may gradually become clear. Here I might see my basic underlying belief, "Life should be free from pain," or "Life should be comfortable." As this belief becomes clear, I label it in the same way. There's quite a difference between thinking, *thus believing*, that life should be comfortable and saying, "Having a believed thought that life should be comfortable."

Although we might label it a hundred or a thousand times, at some point we see that even the most stubborn thought is not necessarily the truth about reality, but just a thought. We might also see that this particular thought has been silently directing our behavior. Here we become aware, where before we were blind. Our blind spots are blind by definition, but with the meticulous application of thought-labeling, the light of awareness begins to clarify the once unseen beliefs that have dictated many of our unskillful behavior patterns.

We often don't realize the extent of our own blind spots, how we don't know ourselves, and all the havoc we create—the unending havoc—with both ourselves and others. We can know all about practice. We can know all about the techniques. But sometimes we underestimate the relentlessness and the honesty that are required to really face the fears out of which all our blind beliefs and behaviors arise.

The problem, in a way, is that we know too much. We certainly think too much. We often talk too much. It's very easy to have knowing, thinking, and talking replace the hard work—the often painful work—of genuine practice. Not to say that practice has to be a dark and grim task. The more honest we are at looking at ourselves, at seeing through our blind spots and cover strategies, the lighter we become. Why? Because in becoming more aware, we can give up our unnecessary baggage—the self-images that we cling to, the pretenses, the someone special we think we need to be.

The first time I met Joko Beck was in a formal interview at a retreat, and I was anxious about how to relate to a famous Zen teacher. I sat down and told her my name. She asked me, "Where are you from?" I immediately froze in fear; I thought she was asking me the ultimate Zen question. When I answered "I don't know," she burst out laughing. She meant "Where did I live?"! I had come in with so many assumptions—about what Zen was, what a famous Zen teacher would be like, who I was supposed to be—and it never occurred to me to inspect these pictures. Because I had not yet learned the value of labeling thoughts, I bought into my pictures as uninspected truths. Since then I have seen time and again how crucial this basic practice of thought-labeling can be in clarifying the countless layers of illusions that silently run our lives.

But sometimes we forget that this process takes time and perseverance. Sometimes we forget about all the basic training we must do, not just in the beginning but throughout the practice life—about how often we have to repeat our efforts, such as with thought-labeling.

Thought-labeling is a primary tool in helping us to see the holes in the Swiss cheese for what they are. As we break our identification with our beliefs, we no longer call them "me." And as we stop believing in each little hole, we relate increasingly from the clarity of the bigger whole. But we must realize that thought-labeling does not come naturally or easily. The precision, honesty, and perseverance required to do this practice meticulously may take years to develop.

Clarifying our belief systems is about becoming aware. But this approach is just part of our basic practice. The second approach, which is equally essential, is more difficult to describe clearly. This second approach can be called *experiencing*. What experiencing is we will touch on throughout this book, in a variety of contexts. Essentially it's an awareness of the physical reality of the present moment. In part it's an awareness of the sensations in the body, including—but not limited to—the sensations of the breath; it's also an awareness of environmental phenomena such as sounds, sights, and smells.

To get a taste of this, become aware right now. What do you feel in your body? Where are your strongest sensations? Pick one sensation: specifically how does it feel? What is its texture? Now become aware of the environment. Are there any sounds? How does the air feel on your skin? Notice how unfamiliar this experiencing of the physical reality of the present moment may be to you. Notice the sense of presence that comes upon leaving the mental world and entering the physical experience of the moment. This experiencing is only possible when we are not caught in thinking.

This two-part approach to practice—clarifying our beliefs and experiencing physical reality—allows us to widen our container of awareness to include even our most difficult emotional reactions to life. We can even learn to relate to our worst fears, our deepest shame, our most unwanted feelings—whatever "holes" we're caught in—in a new way. As we clarify our believed thoughts, no longer taking them as truth, and as we reside in the bodily component of our experience, we begin to see that our experience of these little holes is actually nothing more than a combination of deeply believed thoughts and a complex of subtle and not-so-subtle uncomfortable bodily sensations. Seeing this—and I mean seeing it in the way that fosters real understanding—is a taste of freedom.

As our container of awareness enlarges, we find that we can now be with these little holes while not believing in them quite so solidly. With awareness, our artificial, self-limiting view of who we are becomes more porous. We can then begin to connect with the reality of life as it is. It's like taking off our colored glasses and seeing without the filter of our conditioning, desires, and judgments. It's like taking our foot out of a tight shoe: the sense of restriction and boundary disappears.

But of course, within no time at all, we reclaim our colored glasses and tight shoes. For though we sense the freedom of living with what is, we still prefer our familiar patterns, tight shoes and all! The process of settling into the willingness to just be is slow and halting. Resistance within the process returns again and again. As we practice, we continually struggle between the yes and the no, between residing in the struggle and spinning off toward our illusion of comfort and security.

But somewhere along the way, the gradual shift from unwillingness to willingness may take place. It is this crucial shift, *to the willingness to just be,* that finally allows us to be with life as it is—holes and all. Again, the holes don't necessarily go away; we simply see them for what they are, no longer investing them with solid belief. This transformative process is both the heart and the fruit of practice.

4

Experiencing and the Witness

AS WE EXAMINE THE PRACTICE LIFE, a word that will keep coming up is *experiencing*. What exactly does it mean, to experience? Can we define it? Can we describe it?

Unfortunately, "experiencing" can't be adequately described, and it certainly can't be defined. We have to learn what it means from the inside, as a living reality. At first we might equate it with bringing awareness to particular sensations, such as those of the breath. We focus on the coolness as the breath enters the nostrils or the feeling of the upper body as it rises and falls with our inhalations and exhalations. And bringing awareness to the breath in this focused way grounds us in physical reality. Entering the world of physical reality takes us out of our spinning mental world and provides a taste of experiencing.

But experiencing cannot be reduced to just single sensations, although it is only by starting at this end of the awareness continuum that we can begin to approach the depth and breadth that the process of experiencing can be. Often, on this end of the continuum, we can experience the concentrated states called *samadhi*, in which we become fully absorbed in the object of concentration. By fully focusing on the breath or the light of a candle or sounds (such as chanting or music), we can sometimes even lose our sense of "self." But again, these focused states are only preliminary ones. What is important about them is that they ground us in the physical reality of the moment rather than in our thoughts. However, in terms of experiencing, they are still very limited, in that they are mainly shutting life out. Experiencing always entails being awake and aware, and we can't be awake and aware when we are absorbed in a narrow band of sensory input.

In approaching the gestalt awareness that we call experiencing, many have found helpful the meditation exercise called the Three-by-Three. In this practice you bring three different aspects of sensory input into awareness simultaneously and hold them for three complete breaths. For example, you could first bring awareness to the sensations of the breath and then, while staying with that, begin to include the sense of touch in your hands as they rest in your lap. And then, while staying with awareness of breath and touch, expand your awareness to include the perception of sound, and then hold all three together for three complete breaths.

To get a taste of the Three-by-Three, try this: first bring awareness to the sensations of the breath. Be sure you are feeling the physical quality of the breath, not just the thought of the breath. Now add to awareness the feeling of the air on your skin. Feel the temperature and the texture of the air. Now, while maintaining awareness of the breath and the air, expand your awareness to include the feeling of presence in your posture. Hold these three components—the breath, the air, and the posture—in awareness for three full breaths.

You can do this for several rounds of three breaths, using a variety of focal points: your feet, the top of your head, your mouth, back, or buttocks. You can use sight (shapes, colors, shadows) or any prevailing sensations or tensions in the body. The point is to expand the awareness, *based in physical reality*, and hold it without slipping back into thought. In directing awareness to the three different points of focus, we experience more fully *what is happening right now*. This can be difficult, especially in the beginning, but when you do this exercise over and over, the container of awareness gradually widens. At some point you may experience a literal jump into "witness" space, in which you no longer identify solely with the sense of "me" that is our usual orientation.

In this wider container of the witness awareness, there is a strong sense of attending but not to any particular thing. Awareness simply moves to whatever presents itself to our field of sensations and perceptions. We go beyond intentionally directing awareness, as in following the breath or practicing the Three-by-Three. The awareness moves from one point of focus to another, often attending to several aspects simultaneously. Without attempting to hold any of these aspects as a reference point, we witness the sensory world from a clear, alert perspective. This is "experiencing."

Students often get confused with the different terminology. Certain questions often arise. How does the "observer" fit in? Is the observer the same as or different from the witness? Generally there is no witness, just as there is no observer. These are simply descriptions of different stages in the continuum of widening awareness. The observer is a description of the stage at which we begin observing ourselves as if from outside ourselves. But there is still a strong sense of a "self" who is doing the observing. As we approach the witness stage, we experience a sense of stillness and spaciousness and less sense of a "self" witnessing. It isn't that we are distant from our experience. In fact, in witness awareness, we feel a strong sense of presence and connection. But these descriptions of the continuum of awareness are only theoretical. The point is to experience this continuum for ourselves, from the inside.

One essential aspect of experiencing is that the more we are experiencing, the less we are caught in thinking. The reverse is also true: the more we are caught in thinking, the less we are capable of actually experiencing. That's why the technique of thought-labeling is preliminary and complementary to experiencing: as long as we believe in our thoughts, we remain locked in the mental world, cut off from the physical reality of the moment.

As we practice observing and labeling our own thought patterns, we may begin to notice how they are often directly related to the particular strategies of behavior that we use to cope with everyday life. For example, if our basic strategy is to be in control, we may notice that a lot of our thinking takes the form of planning. We are simply continuing our basic strategy even while meditating. This is no coincidence. If we are driven by the fear of things falling apart, we will do whatever we can to avoid facing this fear. We will even spend our meditation time lost in planning trying to avoid the discomfort of not being in control. The practice is to see this dynamic as clearly as possible. So when we see our repeating pattern—whatever it may be—we label our thoughts so that we don't get lost in them. As we become more familiar with these types of thoughts, we can generically label them "planning" and return awareness to the body. Recognizing that the planning is at least in part a cover for discomfort, we return to the body with the awareness that we may need to feel the discomfort. We will find it easier to actually experience a moment of discomfort when we are not just lost believing in our mental world.

How do your own thinking patterns follow your strategies of behavior? If you spend a lot of time fantasizing while meditating, can you see how it follows the basic strategy of seeking pleasure and diversion to avoid the anxious quiver of being? When this becomes clear, label the thoughts "fantasizing," then return to the physical discomfort out of which the desire to find escape arose. If you tend to get lost in your own drama, reliving or imagining conversations, can you relate this pattern to the strategy of doing whatever is necessary to avoid the fear of being ignored or discounted? In this case the practice would be to label the thoughts "conversing" or "dramatizing" and then return to the physical reality of the "hole" out of which the need to seek validation arose.

The point is, when our thoughts are not clearly seen and labeled, it's very difficult to actually *experience* on a bodily level, because we're believing the thoughts that are filtering through. Occassionally, especially when caught in a confusing or intense emotional reaction, we may have so many thoughts going through our minds that it's difficult to see what to label. Then we can even make up a very generalized thought that, when labeled, will clarify the chaotic mental jumble. For example, when I used to awaken in the early morning hours to unending anxious thoughts, the specific thought contents were not the issue. The thoughts were arising from the need to get control, to avoid the fear of chaos. So I would say, "Having a believed thought: things are out of control; I've got to get control." This specific thought never actually went through my mind. I made it up to summarize and simplify the mental jumble. Identifying and labeling the process allowed me to return to the physical reality of the moment. When we are caught in thinking, our ability to experience the truth of the moment eludes us. The more we observe and come to know ourselves with clarity, the more we can see through our thought patterns, thereby entering the experiential world of the present moment.

But even when we clearly see and label our thoughts, staying in the experiential world is difficult, especially in the early stages of practice. Why, even while sitting in meditation, is it so hard to simply reside in the body? What are we resisting? We have to be honest about this. Often we don't want to stay in the present moment for more than a few seconds.

On the most superficial level, perhaps it's difficult to reside in the experiential world because it's unfamiliar. We're not educated to experience, to be present, to inhabit the sensory world. Most of our formal education involves cultivating the thinking process. As well, our culture is oriented toward fostering security and comfort. So just to counteract our years of conditioning, learning how to be present requires repeated practice.

Furthermore, when we do allow ourselves to reside in the present moment, we often don't like it one bit. We're apt to come into contact with the underlying jangle that I call the anxious quiver of being. We might feel vague sensations of groundlessness or the hole of discomfort at the core of our unhealed pain. We will almost always resist experiencing these places because they don't feel good at all. We move away from the shakiness, back into the false comfort of our thoughts.

This is especially true during powerful emotional reactions. For example, if strong anxiety arises, the intensity of dread can feel like death. Even when we remember to practice—regarding the anxiety as our path, not as something we have to escape— we may have trouble residing in the feeling of anxiety. Labeling the thoughts will help, because we are no longer fueling the emotion with beliefs such as "I can't do this" or "This is too much." But even when we are able to label our thoughts and thereby loosen our attachment to them, we may still resist the physical discomfort of anxiety. We resist because we don't like the discomfort.

But with practice we may eventually discover that these powerful emotions, which can feel like death, are not death. In fact, they are nothing more than a combination of believed thoughts and strong or unpleasant physical sensations. As we cultivate the willingness to just be with the physical experience of the emotion, this fact can gradually become clear to us. With perseverance and effort, we discover that it is possible, through experiencing, to transform our solid emotional reactions into something much more porous. It's not that they disappear (although they might) but that we hold them much more lightly.

For example, there was one period when I was particularly discouraged about my practice life. It felt as if my practice was stagnant, yet I knew that I was unwilling to make the necessary efforts. It reached a point at which I began to seriously question myself, and the discouragement and self-doubt spiraled down into a state of anxiety and hopelessness. I wondered why I should even bother with practice, because nothing seemed to be going right.

I went to see Joko to describe what was going on, and she first asked me what my most believed thoughts were. I realized that I didn't know. In fact, I had forgotten to even attempt to label my thoughts. She also asked me whether I could reside in the physical experience of my emotional state.

For the next few days, whenever the discouragement or anxiety arose, I'd first ask myself what my most believed thoughts were. And as they became clear, I would label them: "Having a believed thought: nothing matters," "Having a believed thought: I'll never be good at this," "Having a believed thought: what's the use?" Often I would have to label the same thought over and over. But once the story line was obvious, it became easier to approach the physical experience of the emotion itself. There was still resistance to the unpleasant quality of the physical experience, especially the physical sensations of doom and anxiety in my midsection. But as I continued to bring awareness to my bodily experience, the density of the emotion began to change. Instead of something solid, the emotion began to break up into smaller aggregates of labeled thoughts and individual, constantly changing, sensations. Even though there was still a residue of sensations, it was no longer what I would normally identify as "discouragement" or "anxiety."

In this example, through the practice of experiencing, we could still feel some anxiety but not *be* anxious. We identify not so much with "me" or "my anxiety" but with the wider container of awareness that we are calling the witness. From this increased spaciousness, there is a stillness within which we can experience what's going on. Our awareness is like the sky, and all the contents of awareness—thoughts, emotions, states of mind—are passing clouds. As we experience our emotions, we come to understand that they are not as dense and substantial as they appear. This thing we call an emotion is just a complex of thoughts and sensations, and like a cloud, it has no substantial reality. But the only way to make this understanding real is through the practice of experiencing itself, whereby we bring awareness to the physical reality of the moment.

What about those occasions when we can, in fact, really settle down in meditation? What about those moments when we experience the pleasant sensations of feeling still, calm, and clear? Why don't we stay there? Why do we leave this present moment when it seems positive? Sometimes the movement away from the present moment is very definite and rapid, as if the present moment were dangerous. What is the danger? As we reside in the present moment, less caught up in our thoughts, there is a loosening of "me-ness." Being without the familiar ground of self-identity can indeed feel dangerous. The more we let loose, the stronger the sense of groundlessness. That we resist at this point, moving back into our thought-based world, is understandable. However, if our aspiration is to become free, we must practice returning to this groundless place.

Why do we have to return? Why, in fact, is it so necessary to be in the present moment? We must return to the present moment because it alone can bring us into contact with what's real. And only by connecting with what's real can we experience the satisfaction in life that all of us are looking for. Even if in the present moment we are caught in fear, the key to freedom lies in experiencing the physical reality of the terror. It is here that our me-ness, our years of conditioning, our unhealed wounds, and the overlay we've constructed to protect them— all of which are rooted in our very cells—can be addressed. Experiencing transforms us because it permeates the seeming solidity of this cellular memory. From the wider awareness of the witness, this tightly knit sense of self, with all its painful and unwanted emotions, begins to unravel. We can then see it for what it is: a complex of deeply believed thoughts, unpleasant sensations, and ancient memories! We stop identifying with this narrow sense of "self" and start identifying with the wider and more spacious context of awareness itself.

Experiencing brings us to the understanding that we are more than just this body, just this personal drama. Our willingness to return to the physical reality of the present moment allows us to connect with Life—unconditioned energy—as it flows through our conditioned body. I'm not talking about some mystical state of consciousness that requires years of meditation in the seclusion of a monastery. I'm talking about the soft effort of cultivating the willingness to just be in the experience of our life as it is. As we practice, we will naturally encounter resistance. We will make judgments like "This isn't working" and "I'll never get it right." As always, the instruction is to persevere—acknowledging the resistance and the judgments for what they are—and to return to the state of residing in experience itself.

5

The Eighty-fourth Problem

ONCE A FARMER WENT TO TELL THE BUDDHA about his problems. He described his difficulties farming—how either droughts or monsoons complicated his work. He told the Buddha about his wife—how even though he loved her, there were certain things about her he wanted to change. Likewise with his children—yes, he loved them, but they weren't turning out quite the way he wanted. When he was finished, he asked how the Buddha could help him with his troubles.

The Buddha said, "I'm sorry, but I can't help you."

"What do you mean?" railed the farmer. "You're supposed to be a great teacher!"

The Buddha replied, "Sir, it's like this. All human beings have eighty-three problems. It's a fact of life. Sure, a few problems may go away now and then, but soon enough others will arise. So we'll always have eighty-three problems."

The farmer responded indignantly, "Then what's the good of all your teaching?"

The Buddha replied, "My teaching can't help with the eighty-three problems, but perhaps it can help with the eighty-fourth problem."

"What's that?" asked the farmer.

"The eighty-fourth problem is that we don't want to have any problems."

Although we may not realize it, we all have the deep-seated belief that if we practice long and hard enough, our problems will disappear. And beneath that hidden belief lies an even deeper one: that life *should* be free from pain. Although these core beliefs are often what brings us to practice, a life free of difficulties is not what practice is about. Practice is about becoming awake to the truth of who we really are. As we live the practice life, our relationship to our problems may, in fact, become less burdened. But as conditioned beings living in a messy world, we will always have difficulties. We will always have eighty-three problems.

Expecting our problems to go away is truly our fundamental problem. We resist facing our life as it is, because facing life as it is means abandoning how we think our life should be. We rarely take a breath without wanting life to be other than it is. This resistance is basic to human life. For the most part, we don't want to wake up. We want to hold on to our beliefs and even to our suffering! We don't want to give up our illusions, even when they make us miserable. One of the challenges of living the practice life is that practice eventually brings up everything we don't want to face. So we resist. This, too, is a conditioned response; it's ego's effort to maintain control; it's fear of giving up the known (even if the known is making us unhappy).

Resistance comes in many forms: not wanting to sit in meditation, choosing to spin off into our mental world, suppressing or avoiding emotional pain, finding fault with ourselves and our lives. No matter what form it takes, resistance brings no peace. Whatever we resist we actually strengthen, because we solidify it, empowering it to stay in our life.

But the opposite is also true. When we begin to cultivate the willingness to be with life as it is, regardless of whether we like it, our relationship to what we've avoided begins to change. Up until now we have probably felt that we had no choice except to push these things away. But as we observe ourselves resisting them, we can see that this pattern simply perpetuates our pain. We begin to see the possibility of softening our hardened stance by bringing the light touch of awareness into those areas where we've never wanted to go. Just having the willingness to look, instead of pushing away, will soften our stance and perhaps even bring a sense of spaciousness within which to experience whatever it is we've resisted.

This reminds me of a story Pema Chödrön tells about a childhood friend who had recurring nightmares in which ferocious monsters would chase her through a house. Whenever she would close a door behind her, the monsters would open it and frighten her. Pema asked her what the monsters looked like, but she realized that she never really looked at them. However, the next time she had the nightmare, just as she was about to open a door to avoid being caught by the monsters, she was somehow able to stop running, turn around, and look at them. Although they were huge, with horrible features, they didn't attack; they just jumped up and down. As she looked even closer, these three-dimensional colored monsters began to shrink into two-dimensional black-and-white shapes. Then she awoke, never to have that nightmare again.

It is the pushing away of our "monsters" that makes them so solid. As we begin to see through the solidity of this resistance, our life becomes more workable. Although we may not like our life as it is, we still don't have to wage war against it. We can start by noticing all the ways that we avoid this moment, all the ways we avoid practice, all the ways we resist. We can see it in virtually everything we do. We can see it in how we don't want to sit, how we don't want to stay with our physical experience for more than a few seconds, how we choose to relentlessly spin off into thinking about the past or the future. We can see it in our commitment to believing thoughts such as "This is too hard," "I can't do it," "I'll never measure up." We see how we're just a well-oiled resistance machine!

It's a fact that resistance is one of the most difficult aspects of practice. Its manifestations can be compelling, and it comes at us in so many different ways. Often, when we experience this difficulty in our practice—that we simply don't want to do it—we make judgments that we then believe. We might conclude that we're a failure or that practice doesn't work. Judgmental thoughts like these might need to be seen clearly and labeled many times before we can unburden ourselves of them. If we can't bring some spaciousness to such heavy, harsh beliefs, we will solidify our resistance even more, strengthening our habitual stances to avoid entering the practice life. However, when we see these thoughts clearly, we can stop judging what we resist as bad. As well, we can stop judging our resisting selves as bad. Instead, we can develop the curiosity that will allow us to turn and face what we've been avoiding. Perhaps we can even welcome each instance of resistance as an opportunity to learn.

When I was finally ready to stop running away from my fears, Joko Beck gave me a practice tool that's proved invaluable in working with unwanted experiences. The practice is to ask the question "What *is* this?" This question is really a Zen koan, because there is no way the answer can come from thinking about your experience. It can only come from actually experiencing it. In fact, the answer is the experience of the present moment itself. In Pema's story, for example, when the friend turns around to look at the monsters, she is essentially asking, "What *is* this?"

Whether resistance manifests as seeking distractions, spacing out, fantasizing, planning, or sleeping—what *is* it? What is it that blocks awareness in the present moment? Take a minute right now to simply be here. Feel any resistance to residing in the moment. Ask, "What *is* this?" How does the resistance feel in your body? What is its essence? Where is it located? What is its texture? Does it have a voice?

Again ask the question "What *is* this?" Try to stay with the experience of it. If you drift away, come back and ask the question again. Stay with the resistance. Go deeper. Is it physical discomfort you're resisting? Is it emotional discomfort? Can you bring to it the light touch of awareness? Can you stay with it for *just one more breath*? Can you enter into the willingness to experience the "whatness" of this resistance?

Until we're willing to fully experience this resistance within the context of a wider awareness, we will continue to flounder in our practice. Only after the endless disappointments of resisting our practice might we be able to enter the willingness to reside in the resistance itself. Only then might we be curious enough to make resistance itself the subject of practice. When we finally begin to reside in our resistance, when we finally start to experience how our protective and comfort-seeking strategies hold us back and close us down, when we begin to face those things we never wanted to face—that's our bridge to living a genuine life. That's when the fruits of practice—a certain sense of freedom, of openness, of gratitude—begin to manifest in our daily lives.

To willingly include whatever we encounter, not to push the unwanted away, is what it means to say "yes" to our lives. But we can't force ourselves to say "yes" any more than we can meaningfully say the popular phrase "No problem!" "No problem!" does have, on a profound level, a real meaning; but it falls far short as long as we hold on to our deep-seated desire not to have any problems. That we'll try to hold on to this desire is a given: it's what humans do. Nevertheless, in living the practice life, our only real option is to persevere in including all of our experience, because our only other option is to keep pushing life away, with all the suffering that that entails.

6

Three Aspects of Sitting

PRACTICE CAN NEVER BE LEARNED just by reading or thinking about it. To awaken clarity based on genuine understanding, we have to learn from our own experience. Nonetheless, it's good to have a clear overview of what sitting practice is, even if it is, in part, conceptual. How often have you realized, right in the middle of a sitting, that you didn't even know what the basic practice was? How often have you asked yourself, "What exactly am I supposed to be doing here?" This confusion is a normal part of the practice path, which is a good reason to review basic sitting instructions regularly.

Meditation practice can be divided into three parts. These three are not really separate and distinct; they are a continuum. For purposes of description, however, we will look at these three aspects of sitting as if they were separate entities.

The first aspect of sitting is *being-in-the-body*. This is the basic ground of practice. When we first sit down to meditate, we take a specific posture. The important point is not which posture we take but whether we're actually present to the physical experience. Being-in-the-body means we're awake, aware, present to what is actually going on. So even though it's true that certain postures are conducive to this level of awareness, it's also true that we can meditate on a subway, standing up, or lying in bed.

It's useful to have a routine to bring awareness to the physical reality of the moment, especially when we first sit down to meditate. For example, when I sit down, I ask myself, "What is going on right now?" Then I touch in with my physical state, my mental/emotional state, and the environmental input (temperature, sound, light, and so on). This check might require only a few seconds, but it immediately takes me out of my mental realm and grounds me in the more concrete physical world. The point is not to *think* about the body, the emotions, or the environment but to actually feel them. After this quick check, I return awareness to the posture by telling myself: "Allow the head to float to the top, so that the lower back can lengthen, broaden, and soften." This reminder brings me further into my bodily experience. Throughout the sitting period, whenever I find myself spinning off into thoughts, I use this reminder to bring my awareness back to the present moment. The essence of being-in-the-body is simply to be here.

Normally, after settling into the sitting posture, I bring awareness to the breath in a very concentrated way for just a few minutes. I am not thinking about the breath but bringing awareness to the actual sensations of its entering and leaving my body. For this brief period, when thoughts arise, I don't label them; I narrow my awareness to focus solely on the experience of breathing. The value of this practice is that it allows me to settle into sitting.

But the value of this (or any other) concentrative practice— that it can shut life out—is also its limitation. Practice is about opening to life, not about shutting it out. And even though continuous concentration on the breath can make us feel calm and relaxed as well as focused and centered, this is not the point of sitting practice. As much as we would like to have pleasing or special experiences, the path of meditation is about being awake. It's about being awake to *whatever* we feel. It's ultimately about learning to be with our life as it is. So although concentration practices can certainly be helpful at times, we aspire to spend most of our sitting time in a more wide-open awareness.

In order to make the transition from concentration on the breath to a wide-open awareness, I usually do a few rounds of Three-by-Three's. This forces me to stay focused and at the same time expand the awareness to become more wide open. Three-by-Three's help to bring a groundedness to practice without which wide-open awareness can tend to be too spacey and amorphous.

Yet, wide-open awareness is the essence of being-in-the-body. This is where we become aware of bodily sensations, thoughts, changing states of mind, and input from the environment. I try to keep about one third of my attention on the breath, to stay grounded, but the basic practice is just to be aware, to simply observe and experience whatever is happening. There is really nothing special about this approach—it is very low key. We're attempting to see and experience life as it arises by letting it just be there—minus our opinions and judgments. Yet, as low-key as this approach is, there is still the never-ending struggle between just being here and our addiction to the comfort and security of our mental world.

So this first aspect of sitting—being-in-the-body—simple as it sounds, is actually very difficult. Why? Because we *don't* want to be here. A strong part of us prefers the self-centered dream of plans and fantasies. That's what makes this practice so difficult: the constant, unromantic, nonexotic struggle just to be here. As we sit in wide-open awareness, however, as the body/mind gradually settles down, we can begin to enter the silence, in which passing thoughts no longer hook us. We enter the silence not by trying to enter, but through the constant soft effort to be present, allowing life to just be.

The second mode of sitting is *labeling and experiencing*. As we sit, emotions arise. Sometimes they simply pass through when we become aware of them. But sometimes they demand our attention. When that happens, we become more focused in our practice. With precision we begin to label our thoughts. As well, we focus on experiencing the bodily state that is an inextricable part of an emotional reaction.

As emotions arise, we can ask, "What *is* this?" The answer to this question is never analytical. It cannot be reached with thought, because it is not what the emotion is about. It's what it is. So we look to our experience itself, noticing where we feel the emotion in the body. We notice its quality or texture. We notice its changing faces. And we come to know, as if for the first time, what the emotion actually feels like.

Invariably we will slip back into thinking. As long as we are caught in thinking, we can't continue to experience the bodily component of our emotions. In fact, the more intense the emotion, the more we will want to believe our thoughts. So the practice is to label the thoughts over and over—to see them clearly and to break our identification with them. It will almost always involve moving back and forth between labeling and experiencing.

Learning to stay with—to reside in—our emotions in this way allows us to see how most of our emotional distress is based on our conditioning, and particularly on the decisions and beliefs that arose out of that conditioning. We come to see that these emotional reactions—which we often fear and prefer to avoid—amount to little more than believed thoughts and strong or unpleasant physical sensations. We can see that when we are willing to experience them with precision and curiosity, we no longer have to fear them or push them away. Thus our belief systems become clarified.

The third aspect of our sitting practice is *opening into the heart of experiencing*. On those occasions when we experience dense, intense, or even overwhelming emotions, when we seem so confused that we don't even know how to practice, what can we do?

When the precision of labeling thoughts is not an option, the practice is to breathe the painful reaction into the center of the chest. Although eventually we will still need to clarify the believed thoughts that are an inextricable part of our emotional reaction, for now we simply open to our deepest fears and humiliations. We pull our swirling physical sensations, via the inbreath, into the center of the chest, allowing the center of the chest to be a container of awareness for our strong emotions. We're not trying to change anything. We're just learning to fully experience our emotions. Why? Because experiencing our emotions fully will allow them to break through the layers of self-protective armor and awaken our heart. Fully felt, our emotions may clear the path to the deep well of love and compassion that is the essence of our being.

It is in these darker moments, when we feel overwhelmed, that we are apt to judge ourselves most harshly. We're likely to solidify the most negative core beliefs about ourselves, seeing ourselves as weak, as losers, as hopeless. It's at this point that we most need a sense of heart, of kindness, of lightness, in the practice. We do this by learning to breathe into the heartspace, thereby undercutting the relentless self-judgment of our deeply held beliefs. As we breathe into this space, piercing our armoring and awakening the heart, we can open into a more benign awareness toward ourselves and the human predicament. We can begin to relate to ourselves as we might relate to a defenseless child in distress—nonjudgmentally, with friendliness, tolerance, and kindness. Our willingness to breathe into the heart, to stay in that space for *just one more breath*, shows us our strength, our courage, to go on.

By opening into the heart of experiencing, we can come to understand that *everything* is workable. This is one of the key points of practice. Our efforts to be in the body, and to label and experience, will inevitably "fail" at times. We will have periods of aspiration and effort, followed by dry spells and apathy. Ups and downs in practice are predictable and inevitable. That we seize these ups and downs as opportunities to judge ourselves as failures or as superstars is the problem. The countermeasure is always to simply persevere—to attend to one more breath, to label one more thought, to experience one more sensation, to enter just one more time into the heartspace. We can then experience for ourselves that it is ultimately possible to work with everything. It may not be possible today, but it is possible. In fact, it may take years of work in all three aspects of sitting practice for this understanding to become real to us.

Until now I've spoken of these three modes of sitting—being-in-the-body, labeling and experiencing, and opening into the heart of experiencing—as if they were distinct from one another. In truth, although each mode does entail a different aspect of practice, they do have one essential thing in common: they all require that we experience this present moment. That's what our practice always comes down to: just being here. By continually allowing the light of awareness to shine on the confusion and anxiety of the present moment, we break the circuitry of our conditioning. This is the slow transformative path to freedom.

PART II

practicing with emotional distress

7
The Substitute Life

AN AMBITIOUS LONG-TIME MEDITATOR comes to see a Zen teacher. As soon as the student sits down, the teacher asks, "What's the basic human problem?" The student ponders this, then answers, "We're not awake." The teacher says, "Yes, but those are just words. You're just thinking." And ringing the bell, he sends the student away.

Perturbed, the student continues to ponder, "What is the basic human problem?", determined to figure it out. A week later he returns. The teacher says, "Well, have you figured out what the basic human problem is?" The student replies, "Yes. The basic human problem is that we think too much. We're identified with our thinking. We believe our thoughts." The teacher answers, "Again, you're just thinking. You have to see the basic human problem in yourself." The student leaves feeling very dejected.

Wanting to find the right answer, the student pulls out all his Zen books to read and study. When he returns to see the teacher, he's almost strutting, he's so sure he knows the answer to this question. Seeing the state he's in, the teacher asks, "What's the basic human problem?" And the student says, "There is no problem!" He's so happy with his answer. The teacher just stares at him and says, "Then what are you doing here?" In that moment the student instantly deflates. His shoulders drop; his head drops; he feels totally humiliated.

Peering at him, the teacher asks, "What are you experiencing right now?" The student, without even looking up, says, "I just feel like crawling into a hole." At this point the teacher says to him, "If you can fully experience this feeling, then you'll understand the basic human problem."

The practice life almost always comes back to dealing with what we could call the basic human problem. But this problem is not an intellectual one. We can't just sit down and figure it out with our minds, the way the student was trying to do. In fact, trying to figure this out intellectually is part of the very problem we're looking at. We have to be able to see and experience this problem from the inside out in order to understand it.

The essence of the basic human problem is that we live a substitute life. From our basic human need for protection, security, and comfort, we've fabricated a whole maze of constructs and strategies to avoid being with our life as it is. And as a consequence of believing in this substitute life we are disconnected from awareness of our true nature, our naturally open heart.

Our substitute life is made of many different constructs: our identities, our self-images, our concepts of what life is, our opinions and judgments, our expectations, our requirements. All these we take as reality. As a consequence of these tightly held beliefs, we develop certain habitual behavioral strategies to deal with life as we interpret it.

All these strategies are based on core decisions that we made early on about who we are and what our life is about. They are decisions we made to help us cope with the many inevitable pains of growing up. Before these decisions are made, we may begin our lives with a sense of basic wholeness, but when we experience even mundane pain, we start to move away from that sense of connectedness. Perhaps we feel that there's some hole inside us that needs filling. Perhaps we even feel the terror of utter helplessness or of being totally alone. When we feel this anxious quiver in our being, our natural instinct for protection kicks in. And from this natural desire for security and comfort, we begin to fill in that hole and cover over that core of pain.

Take, for example, the very young child who experiences the pain of being left in the crib for too long (which might be only thirty seconds). Especially if this happens repeatedly, the child develops certain pictures and begins to make certain decisions about how life is. Maybe she decides that life isn't safe somehow. Based on this belief, the child develops particular behavioral strategies. Maybe the strategy is to withdraw in order to feel safe. Or maybe the decision is that life is too difficult, and the child develops the strategy of trying harder, of doing whatever it takes to cover the inadequacy he feels. Another strategy could be to seek oblivion or to seek love. It could be a strategy of control or aggression or cheerfulness.

In any case, we weave together these core decisions and strategies into a seemingly solid construct that becomes our substitute life. We believe that this thought-based picture of reality is who we are and what life is. The more we believe in this artificial life, the more we move away from "life as it is."

We live in a psychologically sophisticated age, and given our tendency to psychologize, we are naturally drawn to analyze ourselves, to think about ourselves. But as many, many seekers have found, analyzing in itself does not bring us that basic something we're looking for.

Analyzing is not the solution to the basic human problem. Instead, living the practice life means we're willing to look at the extent to which decisions that we made long ago have created a substitute life. We can practice seeing the extent to which the decisions about who we are and how life is color and filter our present experience. We can see how they still hone in on our experience, picking out like radar those aspects of the environment that will confirm the decisions that we have already made.

For example, suppose we've made the decision, very early on, that no one can be trusted. At some point long after making this decision, we find a partner who is pretty trustworthy, someone who demonstrates time and time again how trustworthy he is. But one time our partner does something that suggests that he can't be trusted. With deadly aim we hone in on this instance, saying, "See! I knew you could never be trusted! No one can ever be trusted!" This single experience far outweighs all our positive experiences with our partner, because it's what we've been expecting to see. This is how the decisions that we've made literally shape our experience. They don't just reflect our experience; they color what we take in.

Once we become aware of the core decisions that are running our substitute life, we begin to see how they manifest through every aspect of our experience. If, for example, you see a decision operating in one of your relationships, you can be sure that this decision is also playing some part in your work and probably even in your perception about practice. I was recently with a student to whom I've been talking for a couple of years. She was telling me about some relationship difficulties she was having. After listening to her speak, one sentence after another, I said to her, "Why don't you write these down?" So she wrote them down. Then I said, "Why don't you write down how you perceive your situation at work?" And she wrote that down. Then I said, "How do you look at your situation in practice? What are your basic thoughts about practice?" So she wrote those down. I read what she had written, then handed the papers to her. Her eyes opened wide. Even though she had used different words for each of these three categories, her core beliefs were essentially the same: "I'll never be good enough. Things will never change. What's the point anyway?"

This woman was believing her thoughts as the truth about reality: relationships are like this, work is like this, practice is like this. It was obvious that her core beliefs were coloring and shaping her whole experience. It wasn't work that was impossible, it wasn't this guy who was doing all these things to her, it wasn't practice—it was her preprogrammed beliefs.

The interesting thing about how we perceive and shape our lives through the filter of core decisions made long ago is that we tend to emphasize what is most negative about ourselves. We embrace the negative view of who we are as our deepest truth, as what will never, ever change. Our core belief might be "I'm basically flawed," or "I'll never measure up," or "I'm utterly hopeless," or "I'm not worthy of love." Whatever it is, it has great solidity in our believed thoughts. And because it influences almost everything we think and do, it narrows and restricts our life to one of unhealed pain.

Perhaps you're wondering, isn't this just psychology that we're talking about? What does this have to do with "real" practice? The answer is simple and clear. Many of the barriers to leading a more open, more genuine, more giving life come directly from our psychologically rooted decisions. These decisions are like boundaries—boundaries that disconnect us from awareness of our true nature, our naturally open heart. The practice life is about *seeing through* our boundaries, our artificial separations of mind, our self-images, our "someone special to be." To think that practice is about achieving some permanently enlightened state of mind—stillness or silence or whatever we want to call it—is really just a fantasy about practice. Practice has to include looking at our stuff. Living in this moment means that we're willing to be with *whatever* this moment holds, including all the ways we are holding ourselves back due to decisions we made in the past.

However, unlike a psychological approach, which might be directed primarily toward changing or adjusting ourselves, practice is about *experiencing*. It's about seeing the truth about the "self" who has constructed this substitute life. As we work in this way, we slowly dismantle this notion of a "self." In fact, the most fundamental core belief of all is "I am a me," with all of the consequent core pain of feeling separate. The more we are able to reside in this quiver of separation, the closer we come to seeing through its insubstantiality. This is the process whereby we open experientially into a vaster sense of Being.

But in order to experience this, we must begin to see how all-pervasive our decisions about ourselves are—and how mechanically we use our familiar strategies to reinforce these decisions over and over again. As we learn to recognize the imprint of our core beliefs on almost everything we think and do, we can see how this substitute life has become our reality.

That's what the Zen teacher meant when he said to the student, "If you can really experience what is going on right now, you'll understand the basic human problem." Seeing that his strategy was to try to be on top, to be the "best," to get the right answer, and to gain whatever he could from it, would show the student what his substitute life was about. When the teacher exposed his strategy and the student experienced great disappointment, the possibility opened up for him to understand that dynamic experientially. He could now see what was running his whole life.

Our emotional reactions are always tied to our substitute life and to our core decisions about what life is supposed to be. We all have expectations and requirements of ourselves, of others, of life. When these expectations are not met, we almost always experience disappointment in some form or another. Once we can see this dynamic—and this is where practice most departs from traditional psychology—we can enter into the next phase of practice. That is, we can learn to reside physically in the original hole that our substitute life is meant to cover and protect us from in the first place.

Suppose a man has made the basic decision, "My wife should take care of me." After a difficult day at work, he's looking forward to coming home to his mate so he can unburden himself. But when he walks into the house, he finds his wife knee-deep in her own stuff. And what she wants to do is talk to him about it!

It is likely that this man will react, with some form of anger. Depending on what strategies are habitual for him, he might start blaming her: "Why don't you ever have time for me? This is how it always is!" and things will go downhill from there. Or maybe his strategy is to push the reactive feelings down; suppression is his pattern. Or maybe he has the strategy of martyrdom; he just seethes and wallows in his righteousness.

The strategy we choose is going to be based on reactions. Our reactions are based on our expectations. Furthermore, we always believe in our reaction as "the truth." That's all we see. We rarely even see the difference between our expectations and our behavioral strategies. It's usually one confused mess.

When we can see the relationship among our decisions, expectations, reactions, and strategies—not as the truth but as the fabric of our substitute life—we can then understand what we bring into the situation. In the example above, the whole setup in the first place was the decision "My mate should take care of me." The disappointment came from the basic setup of that expectation. We can understand how this dynamic works only when we really start looking into ourselves—at our own decisions, our own strategies.

Then what we need to do is stop following our particular strategy of behavior. Whether it's to blame the other person, to justify our own stuff, to suppress, to wallow—whatever its flavor—we refrain from following that strategy. This is not to simply modify our behavior, to make us act like a "better" person. It's so we can then experience the actual emotional reaction that we're feeling. But to practice in this way requires the willingness to just be with our experience, even when it's painful.

In this case, suppose the man is experiencing some form of anger. If he really can stay with this experience of anger—hearing the believed thoughts and feeling the sensations of the emotion in his body—it's likely the anger will subside. Another emotion may emerge as he takes the elevator ride deeper into his being; perhaps the emotion of hurt will arise from a layer underneath the anger. Then, staying with that, he might be able to go further down to some deeper layer where he feels grief, a sense of sadness and loss. Staying with that, perhaps he will be able to go even further, touching in with the feeling of the fear that underlies so much of our emotional experience.

It takes repeated efforts to stay with and experience our re- actions in this way. But if we do it, practicing like this will eventually take us back to the original "hole," whatever it is: feeling separate, abandoned, utterly hopeless, full of fear and dread. Only by uncovering and entering this dreaded part of ourselves can we see through the artificial construct of our substitute life and ultimately reconnect with awareness of our basic wholeness.

Are we willing to move out of the fantasy world in which we see practice as some vague and romantic union with silence? Are we willing to do the painful work of looking at what we do, how we react, how we follow mechanical strategies that lead us to close off, shut down, lash out? Once we can clearly articulate our core decisions and basic strategies, the next stage—residing in the hole that these decisions were meant to protect us from—becomes more straightforward and less dramatic. We can see through and experience our "suffering," not as high drama but as just our "stuff"—the energy of deeply believed thoughts and deeply held bodily sensations. Our life then becomes more workable as we discover that what we thought was the deepest, most negative truth about us is not really as solid as we believed.

We can come to see—to experience—that we are not broken, that we were never broken, and that we don't need to be fixed. This is the essence of the practice life: continuing to see through the crippling boundaries that we ourselves maintain with our blind belief in the solid reality of our substitute life.

8

Practicing with Anger

THE PRACTICE LIFE is about learning to live from our true openhearted nature. We have to learn to practice with this big picture in mind, observing what gets in the way of our basic connectedness. What separates us from our open heart? What shuts life out?

Often we lose sight of the bigger picture. The point of practice is not to feel better but to learn and to see. We need to see into our own system, how we leak energy through our habitual reactions and strategies. We have to learn how to stop these leaks, so as not to find ourselves continuously depleted as we deal with daily life.

For example, when we are caught in anger, we are always cutting ourselves off from the bigger picture and from a sense of our basic connectedness. If we could see our angry emotional reactions clearly, it would become obvious that they deplete us and narrow our life. We would see how they are aversions to life, how they separate us and keep us closed.

Yet, in spite of the fact that we hurt ourselves and others with our anger, we hold on to this restricting emotion with a puzzling tenacity. Even as we continue to inflict pain by leaking our energy through angry emotional reactions, even as we narrow our life to one of petty self-centeredness, we continue to indulge in angry thoughts and behaviors with a stubbornness that defies common sense.

What is anger really about? When life is not the way we want it, we react. If we have expectations, we expect them to be met. If we have requirements, we require them to be met. If we have strong desires, we will not be satisfied unless they are fulfilled. Though life is neutral, with no bias toward fitting our pictures of how it should be, we continue to believe that life should go the way we want. And when it doesn't, the result is often anger, in one form or another.

I'm not talking only about big explosions of anger. Even on mellow days, we leak energy through anger, in subtle ways, from morning to night. We can be angry in the form of impatience if we have to wait in traffic at a red light. We can be angry in the form of irritability if our television remote stops working. We can be angry in the form of self-righteousness if someone arrives late. We can be angry in the form of frustration if our team loses. We can be angry in the form of indignation if we feel we are ignored or not appreciated.

Most of the time we don't even see how we leak away energy through anger, how we narrow our life, or how we perpetuate our suffering through our attachment to life's going a particular way. Most of the time we simply follow one of the two characteristic ways we have been taught to deal with anger when it arises.

First, if our conditioning tells us that it's not OK to be angry, we will suppress our feelings. Even when we know this approach is not good for our physical or emotional health, if the conditioning is strong, we will still tend to stuff our anger. Interestingly we continue to do this even in spiritual practice. It is not uncommon for meditators to unskillfully suppress their anger in an attempt to fulfill some ideal picture of how they're supposed to be. But whether we use meditative bypass or other diversions such as food or television, pushing our anger out of awareness does not free us from it. It continues to imprint on us, festering inside as unhealed pain. Whether it visits us as disease, depression, passive aggression, or an explosion of rage, sooner or later it will arise.

The second, more common, way of dealing with anger is to express it. We express it internally through ruminating or wallowing; we express it externally through blame. The point is that our expression always entails *believing* in our reaction, with all the consequent self-justification. We have a forceful determination to be right and to prevail, even if only in our own mind.

Whether we suppress or express our anger, in neither case do we ever clarify it, nor do we really *experience* it. Even when we're caught up in expressing anger, we're rarely in touch with its energy. We're so lost in the juiciness of believing our thoughts and in blaming that we don't experience the anger. In fact, one of anger's functions seems to be that it allows us to avoid facing what's really happening. What are we avoiding? We could be avoiding the more painful emotions of hurt or grief. We could be avoiding facing the core fears that almost always underlie our anger. It's so much easier to be angry—especially when the juices are flowing—than it is to experience hurt or grief or fear. No wonder we spend so much time indulging our anger! But even when we feel the power and juiciness of being angry, of being right, we are still shutting life out and closing our hearts.

How do we practice with anger? First, of course, we have to realize that the very occurrence of anger is our path. Anger arising is a signal for us to point the arrow of our attention inward. It's an opportunity for us to see the ways we keep ourselves enclosed in the protective reactive shell out of which anger is born. It's a cue for us to look at the ways we're wanting life to meet our expectations, requirements, and desires. In order to clarify these pictures, we have to look inside, without self-justification and blame. And we need to do this with unrelenting honesty and precision.

There is a particular practice relating to anger: "Do not express negative emotions." This instruction often causes reaction and confusion. It might seem like just another moral dictate, another way of suppressing feelings we judge to be bad. It's important to understand that the nonexpression of negative emotions is very different from suppression. When we suppress, we don't feel. In fact, even when we physically or verbally express negative emotions such as anger, we rarely experience what we feel. But when we practice not expressing our anger, we can actually *experience* it. Experiencing is about feeling and clarifying the emotional reactivity.

The practice of nonexpression is, in part, a way to avoid creating harm in the world, one of the basic tenets of the practice life. Yet even if expressing causes no harm—for example, we might beat a pillow—it still avoids real experiencing.

In order to experience, we have to abandon blaming and justifying, the powerful protective strategies that prevent us from feeling the pain beneath the anger. This is where thought-labeling comes in. It's difficult work and it takes precision, but even when we're feeling anger, we can do this practice. For example, "Having a believed thought that he's so inconsiderate." "Having a believed thought that no one should have to put up with this." "Having a believed thought that this isn't fair." "Having a believed thought that this isn't right." Until we can label thoughts in this way, thereby breaking the intense identification with our thinking, it will be very difficult to practice clearly with anger.

The second benefit of nonexpression is that we learn to reside directly, *quietly* in the "what" of the emotion. It's not some vague "I'm in touch with anger," or "I'm feeling angry." *Angry* is just a five-letter word; it's a concept. To really feel anger is not vague—it is very specific. So we ask, "What *is* this?" The answer is not analytical, theoretical, or historical. It's the physical "what" of our experience. We can reside in the emotion—really feel it—sensation by sensation. Tightness? Where? What does it feel like? Heat? Pulsing? Pressure? Our awareness flickers back and forth, absorbing more and more information, until the felt-sense of the witness becomes operative. With witness awareness we experience a bigger container, an increased spaciousness, a stillness within which to feel the emotion.

This is the essence of how to practice with anger: First, we become aware of it, remembering it as our path. Second, we refrain from our strategies—of suppression, or self-justification and blame. Third, we clearly see our believed thoughts and label them. And fourth, we experience the anger itself, directly in the body. When we let ourselves experience it, the anger may peak and transform; we may feel a release from the constriction of believing that this emotion is "me." Then we may be able to access deeper layers—of hurt, grief, fear—each stage requiring this same *experiential* process. Our willingness to be with an emotion in this way allows us to stop identifying with it. We see that who we really are is much bigger than the little "me" that we want to believe in.

It's necessary to acknowledge that we often love our anger, even when it makes our life miserable. We often mistake the feeling of power that accompanies our anger as being somehow authentic and self-validating. This is the so-called ego at its work of perpetuating the self-centered dream.

One of the main difficulties in working with anger is that often it arises suddenly or right in the middle of messy and complex circumstances that aren't conducive to a focused attention on the emotion itself. Perhaps the best we can do is to just watch ourselves go through our familiar angry response. Or perhaps we have experienced the same old pain enough to know at least to keep our mouth shut, to refrain from causing further harm. This in itself could be a big step forward.

We have to understand that it's not bad to feel anger; anger is simply our conditioned response to life when it doesn't match our pictures. We only make matters worse by adding to the anger self-judgment and self-hatred, both of which are rooted in *more* pictures of how we, or life, *should* be. Instead, we can

bring loving-kindness—the essence of which is nonjudgment—
to our practice, lightening the heaviness and self-importance of
our own drama.

To practice with anger, we have to be willing to work with it,
not as the enemy, not as the ancient burden of "my suffering,"
but as just the stuff of our conditioned life. When we see this
clearly, we also see that not visiting our anger on others is a
very big step in learning to clarify it. Learning to keep our
mouth shut when we would otherwise vent is no small task.
This is not to suppress, but to put our potentially harmful
behavior on hold for the time being.

Then, as time allows, we can revisit what actually happened.
When we next sit down to meditate, we can *re-create the upset*
in our mind. We all do this anyway when we wallow and self-
justify, but I'm talking about doing it as practice, intentionally
and with awareness. When we deliberately re-create an upset,
we remember what actually happened—where we were, what
was said, how we felt. If it's difficult to access the same emotional punch, we can exaggerate the circumstances simply to
reconnect with the original feelings. The point is to experience
the anger (or any emotion) within a practice environment. Even
if we can't re-create the exact emotional reaction, we can still
work with it in a way that would not have been possible in the
confusion and speed of the original episode.

One helpful tool that I learned from Joko is to break down
the re-created emotional experience into three components:
the objective situation, the emotion itself, and the behavioral
strategy that followed the emotional reaction. This helps bring
clarity to the process.

For example, your mate or coworker criticizes you, and
before you know it, you're in an angry exchange. Later, when
you re-create this experience, you first ask yourself, "What was
the objective situation? What actually happened?" Often all
that happened is that words were spoken, or even more objectively, sounds connected with the tympanic membrane in your

ear. The words themselves had no emotional load. You grafted the emotional reaction onto the objective events. Once you see this, you can then look at the second component: the emotional reaction itself. What specific emotion or emotions did you feel? Be as precise and honest as you can in identifying your feelings; often we don't even know what they are. Then move to the third component, the behavioral strategy. What was your strategy—to comply, to attack, to withdraw? Though the strategy is not the same as the reaction, they are often connected in the same predictable pattern.

When we're caught in the behavioral strategy, we have little hope of clarifying our anger. This is especially true if our strategy entails blaming and self-justifying, with that accompanying sense of power in being right. If we can refrain from blaming, we can focus on the initial reaction itself. We first ask, "What are the believed thoughts?" Sometimes the believed thoughts are right on the surface; other times they may not be accessible. Either way, the next and most crucial step is to enter the physical experience of the emotion. Truly residing in our anger has the potential to take us down to the core fears that are often driving our surface reactions. Practicing this way repeatedly will enlarge the sense of spaciousness around our angry reactions. As we regard them less as "me," we become less likely to get caught up in them.

For the last several years, I have been doing a practice I find highly effective in working with anger. One day a week I devote the entire day to practicing what I call "nonmanifestation of negative emotions." From the moment I wake up until I go to sleep, I make a conscious effort not to express negative emotions, either externally or internally. This is not just another dictate designed to induce moral behavior. In fact, its effectiveness has nothing to do with that. The reason it's so effective is that it allows me to see the root of anger itself. Because I'm attuned to not expressing the anger, the moment it begins to arise, awareness is likely to kick in. I can see that point at which I would normally choose to believe my thoughts, fueling the expression of the anger. But I can also choose not to attach to the thought, which denies it solidity. I'm practicing not identifying with the notion of "me"—its wants, its judgments—but rather with a more spacious sense of the moment. This is where I can reside directly in the physical manifestations of the anger, in the "what" of anger itself. Sometimes the anger then quickly dissolves, leaving little residue.

For example, recently a policeman stopped me for sliding through a stop sign. I was immediately ready to defend myself with righteous indignation. I felt the heat rising and the adrenaline starting to flow. But I remembered that it was my day to practice not expressing negative emotions. Instantly I saw how I was about to defend my thoughts, my "self." I also felt the layer of fear—fear of losing control. I experienced, *in my body*, what was transpiring, and chose to go the other way. When the policeman started writing up the ticket, I was actually able to be pleasant.

When we see clearly how anger arises simply because life is not fitting our little pictures, dropping the anger is not so difficult. What is difficult is that we want to be angry. But this one-day practice helps us realize what is possible. We can see how our anger comes from our unfulfilled pictures *and* from our wanting to justify the anger. We can also see that when anger arises, we don't have to express it, nor do we have to justify it by defending the believed thoughts.

Sometimes we might have the thought that we must be angry to engage in life. We might think that certain situations require action and that unless we are angry, we won't act. When we see what we think is clearly an injustice, isn't our anger the catalyst for our actions to remedy the situation? If we weren't angry, what would motivate us to create positive change?

From a practice point of view, anger is never justified, no

matter how righteous we may feel. This doesn't mean that we shouldn't act when the situation requires action. It means we can act without the negative aspect of our anger. As long as we fuel this negativity by believing in our thoughts, we impede ourselves from acting with clarity. As long as we are being run by the powerful negative energy of anger, we are closing our hearts tightly shut. In most cases we are still mainly in the grip of fear, in which we make life—whether in the guise of a person, a group, or an institution—the enemy. This roots us firmly in a narrow sense of "self." When we justify our anger in this way, we have lost all sight of the bigger picture, of our basic connectedness.

Once, as the overseer on a large project, I was severely criticized for my work. Even though it was clear to me that objectively the criticism was not justified, it still triggered a strong emotional reaction. And even though I remembered to practice immediately, the negative energy of the anger was unrelenting. I tried the practice of saying "yes" to rejection, inviting the hurt and fear in, but my mind kept spinning off in blame and self-justification, protecting and defending my sense of "self."

The second day I changed my practice, following the dictate "Absolutely no blame or justification." I made this practice my god. I saw that unless I made a strong effort to cut the thinking, the anger would continue to be fueled by the believed thoughts. Over and over again the thoughts arose, wanting to justify my position. Over and over again I cut them off, returning to my physical sensations of heat and queasiness. As the day wore on, I was able to reside in the bodily experience for longer periods. It then became possible to invite the hurt, the rejection, the fear into my awareness, without slipping back into blame. I breathed the feelings directly into the heartspace, allowing them to penetrate my shell of protection.

By the end of the day, the negative energy of the anger was gone. However, there was still a situation to deal with that involved a lot of money and many practical considerations. But without the negative aspect of the anger, I was clear and resolved on what needed to be done. Had I not worked so intensely with my own reaction, there is little doubt that a closed-hearted encounter would have ensued, to no one's benefit. As it was, the resolution was quick and also quite genuine. There was a sense of coming together that seemed to include the bigger picture.

As we enter deeply into practicing with anger, we can develop a sense of spaciousness even in difficult situations. As awareness enlarges around that narrow sense of "me," perhaps we can get a glimpse of what it means to transform our anger, redirecting the energy of anger into the strength of resoluteness, without the negative overlay. This resoluteness engages life with both action and a sense of clarity. Here our self-will—our wanting life to be a particular way—is transformed into strength of purpose and direction, with a clearer understanding of what our life is about. Perhaps in the process we can even begin to serve life rather than always wanting it to serve us. But as long as we are caught in the emotional negativity of anger, the kindness and compassion that we are—our naturally open heart—will not be accessible.

So notice your anger whenever it arises. Regard it as your path to awakening. See how it arises out of your unfulfilled pictures. Notice whether you stuff it or express it. If you express it, notice your flavor: do you express it internally through stewing, or do you put it out there, even in subtle ways? See whether you can identify your believed thoughts. Then bring yourself back to residing in the physical experience of anger itself. Be open to experiencing your core fears. Remember, you can do this only when you choose to stop blaming. Do you want to keep your heart closed in anger? Feel the pain of continuing to live in that way and let that disappointment penetrate your heart.

9

Practicing with Fear

MUCH OF THE PRACTICE life is about dealing with fear. Fear tells us to close down, not to go beyond the protective outer edge of our cocoon. But by giving in to fear, we make it more solid. We strengthen our cocoon, contracting and limiting our existence. Fear has us avoiding some terrible imagined outcome, yet the substitute life we experience by giving in to our fear is already a terrible outcome.

A good friend of mine, Eliot Fintushel, wrote a science fiction novel called *Please Don't Hurt Me*, which features extraterrestrials. Whenever they greet each other, instead of saying "Hello," they say, "Please don't hurt me." Isn't this is an accurate description of the subliminal undercurrent of fear that runs our lives?

Considering how much fear we all have, it's a wonder we're not already experts on this subject. But fear is one of the most slippery realms in life and in practice. The list of what we're afraid of is very long. Our most basic fears include the fear of disease, the fear of pain, the fear of losing control and being helpless, and the fear of the unknown. We may also fear the loss of loved ones and the loss of status and material security. In addition, we're afraid of being criticized and of looking foolish. We're afraid of death and maybe even more afraid of dying. The strongest fear of all may be the fear of fear itself.

There are many other fears that afflict us individually, depending on how our personality has developed. These include the fear of intimacy, the fear of sex, the fear of confrontation, the fear of betrayal, the fear of loneliness, the fear of responsibility, and so on. The first stage of practicing with fear is to gradually become aware of how much fear there is in almost everything we do—the fear behind much of what we call kindness, the fear in our ambition, in our depression, and of course in our anger. We could even define anger as inexperienced fear.

Many of our personality strategies are motivated in one way or another by fear. But often we're not aware that fear is playing a part in what we're doing. Often fear is covered over with anger or contempt. Often we numb it out with activity or diversions. This certainly was the case for me when I was in high school and college. If someone had asked me then about fear, I might have said, "Well, I don't really have much fear. Fear isn't my problem." In those days I loved to party, I loved to dance, and I loved to drink. My goal was to have a good time, and being quite popular, I thought I was very much on top of things. For some time afterward, I regarded this as my best period.

But several years ago, I had a telling insight into my early relationship with fear. As I was listening to an "oldie but goodie" from the early sixties, I had a nice, bittersweet feeling of nostalgia. But in the middle of this nostalgia, I felt an agitation in the pit of my stomach that I recognized as anxiety. I thought, "Why would I have anxiety remembering my 'Golden Age,' when everything was supposedly great?" Then I realized that I was remembering, on a cellular level just from hearing this song, something that had been happening within me all along: anxiety. This anxiety had probably been motivating me to frantically have fun and seek diversions. But I wasn't really aware of it then.

Not until my early twenties did I start becoming aware of my fear. Also around that time I started practicing. I quickly moved to the second stage of practicing with fear, which is to try to get rid of it. Seeing my fears and how they were constricting my life, I took the time-honored path of trying to eliminate them—to confront them, to struggle with them, to overcome them and become free. Such a noble and worthy enterprise! Yet because this approach is often the result of our typical upside-down way of thinking, the practice of confronting our fears in the hope of getting rid of them is usually limited and misdirected.

Since I didn't know this then, I started doing one thing after another to work with my fears by conquering them. For example, I would go out on the street and beg for money, or I would go into stores and ask for food. To ask people for money or food was difficult for me because I saw myself as a well-bred, nice, responsible person who was very independent and would never ask anybody for anything. There was a lot of fear and intimidation around behaving in ways that challenged this self-image.

When I was twenty-five, I joined a Gurdjieff group in San Francisco, where I was assigned a task I would never have undertaken on my own: to make up a song and sing it on Fisherman's Wharf. In the summertime on Fisherman's Wharf, there are hundreds of tourists milling around, waiting to ride on the cable cars. My task was to sing for them. In other words, I was to purposefully make a fool of myself.

I was to sing the Bob Dylan–like song that I had made up in front of all those people and then ask for money by holding out my hat. I dressed up in a hippie outfit with a black derby hat. Not only was I not a hippie, I didn't even like hippies. And I certainly didn't want to be seen as one.

Even now I can remember standing there, petrified, trembling, thinking I was going to faint or throw up. But I sang the song because I had willpower and because I wanted to get rid of my fear. I didn't want to be afraid; that was my motivation. So I sang my song and asked for money. Then, a little while later, I did it again. Each time I did this, it became easier. I realized I was beginning to enjoy doing it. I was having fun. What I didn't realize is that I was just replacing one conditioned self with another. I had replaced this fearful self with one who was now confident in this situation. Nor did I see that through this practice I was not really working with the roots of fear; I was working with the content of fear. When you're working with fear by trying to get rid of it, the content of fear can be endless.

But at that point I didn't understand this. So for the next several years I practiced with fear by trying to get rid of it. I decided I needed a job that would force me, on a daily basis, to go against the fearful patterns I wanted to eradicate. Having worked as a teacher and a computer programmer, I got a job as a carpenter, which was quite a leap into the unknown. For one thing I weighed only 120 pounds and had no physical skills. I would have to go out every day into a new situation that would stretch my natural limits. The truth is, I did have to go into new and threatening situations every day for a couple of years. Then it gradually got easier.

Again, even though this was a valuable practice in other ways, it didn't address the root of fear. Instead, I was working with one content after another; I was not working with the "whatness" of fear. Although I was becoming stronger, I was replacing one self (a conditioned fearful self) with another self (a conditioned self that was free from fear but only in a particular situation). This approach is limited because it doesn't help us dispel the false pictures of who we are.

I began the third stage of working with fear in my early thirties, when I officially became a Zen student. For the most part, I put aside my direct assault on fear and instead came at it indirectly. I learned how to focus on the breath and how to develop strength in the area below the navel called the *hara*. I think I had the hazy, somewhat idealized notion, so typical of many meditation students, that if I sat long and hard enough, I would somehow become free from fear. After all, since fear is just delusion, why bother with it? If I simply concentrate on the breath or the mantra or the ten thousand bows, fear will take care of itself. Yet these practices, despite their seductive appeal and obvious effectiveness in some areas, still do little to address the nature of fear itself.

I experienced another version of this third stage of working with fear several years later at a month-long intensive practice period during which there arose a situation that produced a great deal of fear. The practice that I started doing then was to breathe the energy of my fear directly into the hara. I was trying to transform my fear, trying to turn its energy into strength. In fact, my hara became very strong, in a particular way. However, even though this practice helped me get through a difficult month, I was still not really dealing with fear; I was still trying to get rid of it. Like the other practices, this one was limited because it did not help me see through the notion of my fear-based identity.

Several months later I became severely ill. For about eight months, I was dealing with a whole new realm of fear. As the illness progressed, with the possibility of there being no cure, my fears began to multiply. First was the fear of discomfort, which I clung to, projecting into the future the fear of escalating, uncontrollable pain. Then there was the fear of being dependent on other people as well as the fear of being isolated and alone. Beneath the layers of self-pity and depression, there was the fear of the helplessness of the loss of control. In addition, I was afraid of losing my life as I had known it. I was changing from a healthy and active person into someone who might no longer have the capacity to be physically active. My practice of bringing awareness to the breath and into the hara was of no use because I didn't have the energy or the strength to focus my attention. At this point I spent most of my time wallowing in fear, with little clarity about how to practice with it.

Feeling desperate, I decided to call Joko Beck, whom I had met a few months earlier. After listening to my story, she said something like, "Ezra, I know that this illness isn't pleasant and that you don't like it, but what you have to see is that it is your path." This one remark somehow turned everything right-side up. Perhaps for the first time in my life, I felt willing to allow the fear in, to just let it be without pushing it away. This is the beginning of the fourth stage of practicing with fear, which is to stop seeing it as the enemy or obstacle, but to willingly let it in.

However, as I recovered, this process was still not clear to me. So I began to return to my former way of meditating— focusing on the breath and trying to achieve some tranquil state. This tranquillity was not to be, for as I returned to a somewhat stable physical condition, intense feelings of fear began to arise. Now I was studying with Joko on a regular basis, learning what was to become a very different orientation both to practice and to working with fear. She asked me to look at the fear as a scientist might, with the curiosity of just wanting to discover what it is. The practice, whenever fear arose, was to ask simply, "What *is* this?" The answer always lies in the physical experience of the moment.

Because the emotional agitation from fear is painful to experience, we have an aversion response. Who wants to reside with pain and discomfort? We try to escape it, overcome it, or smash through it. At the same time we often add a whole new negative aspect, experiencing anger and shame at ourselves for feeling afraid. But what about seeing the fear as just another aspect of our conditioned mind? It's not that we're bad people because we experience fear. Fear is simply what is happening as a result of our conditioning. And since this is what's happening, we could decide to really look at it by asking "What *is* this?" The "what" of fear, as with all emotions, has two main components: thoughts and bodily sensations. Just the willingness to stay with the fear, to be curious about the fear, is a big step from pushing it away or trying to overcome it. Cultivating the willingness to be with fear is a step toward learning the willingness to be with our life as it is.

Upon asking "What is this?" we begin to hear the fear-based thoughts that scream through our minds: "I can't do this,"

"What's going to happen to me?" "This isn't how it's supposed to be," "Please stop." We hear also the voices of self-condemnation: "I'll never be good enough," "I'm hopeless," and so on. The practice is to see these thoughts as thoughts, even though they seem so solid. Then we drop into the bodily experience of fear, with all its unpleasant sensations: agitation in the stomach and chest, narrowing of perceptions, tightness in the shoulders, rigidity in the mouth, queasiness, weakness.

By allowing ourselves to be afraid, we come to realize that this horrible feeling of dread is just a combination of some strong physical sensations and some deeply held beliefs about ourselves. The problem is not so much these sensations and thoughts, but our resistance to feeling them. Our desire to avoid fear, our negative attachment to it, is what makes us feel so awful. This is the tight fist of fear—we hold on so tightly to avoid feeling fear that we close off our hearts.

When we are willing to let the fear in, relating to it as a "what" instead of as "me," it loses its juice. We see that even though we may feel terror, there is no real physical danger. Instead of fighting fear with panic or pushing it away, we let it in. We give up our fear of fear. Courage is not the absence of fear; courage is and grows out of the willingness to experience fear. This is where the tight fist of fear begins to open—and we reconnect with our hearts.

The experience of residing in fear is never a clear-cut progression. For me, during intense periods of fear, it was a moment-by-moment struggle. One moment I would want to run away, to push away the fear; the next moment I would want to smash through it. There would also be moments of surrender, when I could say "yes" to it and almost embrace it. Finally I began to see that fear is not solid, that it is nothing more than strong sensations and disabling thoughts based on our conditioning.

When we are willing to let fear in—which is the fourth stage of practicing with it—we discover that we can have fear but not be afraid. When fear arises, instead of "Oh, no!" we learn to say, "Here it comes again. What will it be like this time?" And what happens? The solidity and power of our fear gradually dissipate.

When we can willingly stay with our experience of fear without suppressing it, expressing it, wallowing in it, or judging it, our awareness becomes a wider container. Within that still container, fear's thoughts and sensations can move through us. That's how the practice of awareness can release and transform the frozen mass of emotion-thought that we call fear. As we become familiar with our fear, compassion naturally arises, lightening the whole struggle. It is here that we bring a sense of heart into our practice.

When fear is experienced in the present moment, minus our beliefs and judgements about it, we will find that it is rarely unbearable. In fact, when we really stay present with the physical experience of fear we might experience a deep and pervasive peace, sensing the spaciousness and love that flower as fear transforms on its own. As the solidity of fear becomes porous, life's intrinsic essence simply flows through.

The price we pay for opening up, of course, is the risk of facing exposure to some perceived danger. Although we're not always willing to pay this price, in this fourth stage of practice, our willingness to be with fear becomes stronger. We can practice with all levels of fear, from the big one that arises when we get bad medical news to the midrange fear we feel when we have an unexpected expense to the small, almost unnoticed fear we experience on making an unpleasant telephone call. We start to notice more and more where we just seek comfort or escape, and we slowly learn to see each instance of fear as yet another opportunity to practice.

This is the fifth stage of practicing with fear—seeing it as a signal to look at where we're stuck, where we're holding ourselves back, where we can open to life. For example, can we see the degree to which fear plays a part in our achievements, where we're trying to avoid the fear of feeling unworthy? Or if we examine our relationships, can we see how often we are trying to avoid the fear of rejection, or of being unappreciated or unloved? Can we use these situations to willingly move toward our fears, which will certainly require being open to the unknown? To really experience what fear is, we can't still simultaneously wish for it to go away. We can't even call it "fear"—which is just a conceptual filter between us and our experience.

In the fifth stage of practicing with fear, we may choose to confront our fears. In fact, we may even seek them out. But no longer will we hope to overcome or be free from them in the conventional sense. Rather, we will aspire to simply know the truth of fear, to come to know what lies beyond our protective cocoon.

Frequently I devote one day where I commit myself to the practice of saying yes to fear. What this means is that upon feeling even a hint of anxiety, I practice moving toward the fear, not with the heaviness of "my suffering" but rather with a certain lightness of heart that comes from seeing fear as nothing more than the human conditioning to which we all are subject. Without this lightness of heart, how could we ever step beyond the protective cocoon?

The transformation of fear does not mean that we no longer have fearful responses. It means that we no longer believe that those responses are who we are. This is what practice is about: learning to stop believing that our deep-seated reactivity is who we are. Who we really are is much bigger than any of our fear-based conditioned responses. When we can really experience fear, we see through this false identification, perhaps even glimpsing a vaster sense of Being.

My own practice path with fear continues. I certainly am not free from fear, nor even from the belief that I should be free from fear. But for the most part, I no longer live from the life-long tunnel of fear that was running me. That tunnel seemed so real for so long, I don't think I ever really believed I could be free from it. Considering the length of time I've been working with this, I guess I'm a slow learner. But I've also been a persevering one. Looking back, I now see that there were no mistakes: the clouded understandings and the misdirected efforts are all a necessary part of the practice life.

When fear arises for me now, along with the mind's desire for it to go away, there is also an almost instant recognition of what is going on. Do I try to let it go? Rarely. That would be just another way of trying to get rid of it, of trying to avoid my life. Instead, I breathe into the heartspace, inviting the fear in with a willingness to feel its texture, its whatness. But at the same time, I know that it is not me. My heart could be pounding and my stomach feeling queasy, which are simply the conditioned responses to perceived danger. But there is also a lightness, a spaciousness, through which the conditioning of fear can be experienced. With awareness, the solidity of fear becomes porous. And what remains? Simply life itself, with an increasingly vast sense of being.

IO

Practicing with Pain and Suffering

JEAN-DOMINIQUE BAUBY, the former editor in chief of the French magazine *Elle*, wrote a book called *The Diving Bell and the Butterfly*. This man had lived a very active and creative life, until one day in 1995, when he was only forty-three years old, he experienced a massive stroke that resulted in a rare condition called locked-in syndrome. While his whole body was totally paralyzed, his mind was completely functional. After lying in bed for months, he discovered he could still flutter his left eyelid. With this discovery he devised a form of communication, whereby the number of movements of this one eyelid would signify the different letters of the alphabet. This is how he spelled out each word, each sentence, of his book, poignantly chronicling his thoughts and feelings as he lay locked in his body. He died two days after the book was published.

In the one-page chapter entitled "My Lucky Day," the author describes how the alarm clock connected to his feeding tubes was ringing continuously for half an hour. The intensely piercing *beep beep beep* sound jackhammered into his brain. As he began sweating profusely, the sweat unglued the tape over his right eye, loosening his eyelashes to scratch his pupil. Then his urinary catheter fell out, leaving him soaked in his own urine. There he was, lying in the drenched bed with the piercing sounds and the irritated eye. At that moment a nurse came in and, oblivious to him, switched on the television. What he saw on the screen were the bold letters of a commercial asking, "Were you born lucky?"

The author relates this story without a trace of self-pity. It's primarily a description of his thoughts and sensations. To really appreciate the story, all we have to do is imagine ourselves in the same situation. What would our reactions be?

In general, we don't want to have very much to do with pain. Most living creatures share this aversion. It appears to be a natural and even intelligent part of the evolutionary process. Yet human beings seem unique in their ability to contort from their pain into the state that we commonly call suffering.

Suppose my mate leaves me. There is a hole inside—unmistakably painful—heavy with fear and longing. The beliefs go spinning around: "No one will ever be there for me." "Why is life so hard?" "What's the point, anyway?" And of course, my natural impulse is to resist residing in the painful hole of rejection and loneliness. Unmistakably there is suffering.

How did the pain turn into suffering?

What is actually happening in the moment?

Or suppose one day I wake up feeling sick all over. The days turn into weeks, the weeks turn into months, and the pain and discomfort become more and more debilitating. The mind cries out, longing for relief. "Why is this happening to me?" "This is too much to bear." "What will become of me?" Naturally there is a great resistance to the physical pain and discomfort. And unmistakably there is suffering.

But how did the pain turn into suffering?

And what is actually happening in the moment?

The process starts with our natural tendency to avoid pain. This is a fact of life: we don't like pain. We suffer because we marry our instinctive aversion to pain with the deep-seated belief that life *should* be free from pain. In resisting our pain by holding this belief, we strengthen just what we're trying to avoid. When we make pain the enemy, we solidify it. This resistance is where our suffering begins.

Again, on experiencing pain, we almost always immediately resist. On top of the physical discomfort we quickly add a layer of negative judgments: "Why is this happening to me?" "I can't bear this," and so on. Regardless of whether we actually voice these judgments, we thoroughly believe them, which reinforces their devastating power. Rather than see them as a grafted-on filter, we accept them, unquestioned, as the truth. This blind belief in our thoughts further solidifies our physical experience of pain into the dense heaviness of suffering. And though we can intellectually accept Buddha's first noble truth that life entails suffering, when it happens to *us*, we rarely want anything to do with it.

How do we live the practice life when we're in pain? To apply such phrases as "Be one with the pain" or "There is no self!" (and therefore no one to suffer) is neither comforting nor helpful. We must first understand that both our pain and our suffering are truly our path, our teacher. While this understanding doesn't necessarily entail liking our pain or our suffering, it does liberate us from regarding them as enemies we have to conquer. Once we have this understanding, which is a fundamental change in how we relate to life, we can begin to deal with the layers of pain and suffering that make up so much of our existence.

In early 1991 I had an acute and prolonged relapse of an immune system disease in which my muscles attack themselves. The main physical symptoms were great muscle weakness, painful flulike feelings—as if my cells were polluted—and worst of all, pervasive and relentless nausea. Fortunately the nausea did not result in vomiting, but it was nonetheless very unpleasant. Within two weeks these physical symptoms had been supplemented by classical psychological symptoms: anger, self-pity, depression. I felt tremendous helplessness. I also felt hopelessness—the fear of being forever shut off from life. I didn't want to complain, but I also felt isolated because I didn't know how to communicate what I was feeling. I felt guilt, because I couldn't fulfill my duties. I felt a sense of shame, in the misguided belief that the illness perhaps resulted from my own inadequacies. Although I didn't consciously believe I was dying, the fear of death was definitely powering these other feelings. Beyond even that, I felt fear of the pain of dying, fear of the total loss of control, and even fear of dying in fear.

On the one hand, I had definitive and objective physical symptoms with which to deal. On the other, I had layer upon layer of dark, emotion-based thoughts. These strongly believed thoughts not only exacerbated the physical symptoms but also had their own painful quality. Right in the middle of this, my closest friend of twenty-five years died suddenly and unexpectedly of a heart attack. Despite my years of meditation, I was not prepared to deal with all these circumstances. I felt devoid of a spiritual anchor. This was when I first called Joko and received her pointed yet compassionate advice to see illness and suffering as my path. Joko also mentioned that I might find Stephen Levine's book *Healing into Life and Death* helpful.

My understanding of this idea that we need to see our difficulties as our path changed after that phone call. My belief had been that I couldn't practice *because* my life was so difficult. To accept these difficulties as my practice would mean I'd have to stop resisting and willingly let them in. For whatever reason it was my good fortune to be able to hear Joko's words and literally take them to heart. Years later, in reflecting on these events, I thought of Thomas Merton's words, "True love and prayer are learned in the moment when prayer has become impossible and the heart has turned to stone."

After talking to Joko, I began reading Stephen Levine's powerful and comprehensive book on practicing with illness. I began doing five different meditations a day and continued this for almost two years. Over time I learned to see the difference between the physical pain, the resistance to the pain, and the layers of emotion-based thoughts. I began to see the physical symptoms of discomfort as if they were in the center of a circle, with a concentric layer of resistance around it, and a concentric layer of emotions and thoughts around that.

Since the episodes of nausea were unrelenting, that particular symptom provided a vast laboratory for my practice. Bringing awareness to the nausea over and over, I saw clearly several particularly powerful thoughts that were making up the outer ring of this circle: "I can't take this," "What's going to happen to me?" and "Poor me." I practiced clearly seeing and repeatedly labeling these thoughts as they arose. "Poor me" may not sound like a big deal, but I can't overemphasize the power of this mostly wordless emotional state. And the very intensity of the emotional reaction "I can't take this" is enough to tell us that we are caught in a belief system.

Without awareness these beliefs slip by so easily that we don't even question their truth. With awareness the thoughts can eventually be seen as thoughts and nothing more. In fact, we can begin to realize that they may not even be true! Thus the suffering is no longer fueled by our blind acceptance of our beliefs as the truth about reality.

Once I clarified these beliefs, it was easier to bring awareness to the resistance itself. Acknowledging the resistance as a physical, sensory experience is a big step. No longer seeing it as the enemy ("The Resistance"), we can begin the process of gradually softening into the sensations of resistance themselves. We bring awareness to wherever we experience tightness, pushing away, holding. We soften those energies with the light touch of awareness, opening the edges around the pain.

At first going directly into our pain may not even be an option. In the beginning I certainly couldn't encounter my nausea head-on. But gradually approaching the pain from the edges made a more direct approach possible. No longer believing the thoughts, no longer fighting the resistance, left me with just the physical sensations of nausea. But now it was a physical experience without the suffering! I saw clearly how we hold our suffering in place with fear-based thoughts that arise in reaction to pain. These thoughts are further solidified by our resistance to letting the pain just be.

As often as I was able, I would breathe into the heartspace on the inbreath and then send loving-kindness to my body, to my immune system, via the outbreath. With this sense of spaciousness and heart, I found I could enter directly into the sensations of nausea. In the moments when I could experience the nausea not as "pain" but as intense physical energy, I was struck by a sense of quiet joy. Sometimes I felt a depth of appreciation that, by any ordinary standards, would simply not compute. Opening to pain itself may still not be possible if the pain is intense, but in most cases pain is not as unbearable as we *think* it is. Although the sensations may remain unpleasant, it is often possible for us to actually experience them. Occasionally bringing a softening awareness to the pain can even neutralize the sensations.

Certainly we can't always transform pain from meaningless suffering into a sense of spaciousness, but at least we can practice seeing into the layers of beliefs and resistance that hold our suffering in place, thereby coming closer to gently opening to what is. But seeing into the layers of beliefs and resistance is often difficult, because our conditioning can go very deep. Yet, left unexplored, these beliefs that are most deeply hidden are the very beliefs that silently run our lives. For example, how many of us, when we get seriously ill, engage in what is commonly known as "the battle against illness"? Even when we understand how to practice with discomfort, it is still easy to get caught in the false belief, so prevalent even today, that we "create our own illness" and that with clearer practice we can "defeat" it. Almost all of us believe on some level that physical symptoms imply a gap in our practice. We have the deep-seated view that if we practice long enough and hard enough, we'll see through our problems. Underneath this view is the even more hidden belief that life should be (or can be) free from pain. Yet the Buddha's basic teaching is that pain simply is.

The hidden belief that if our practice is strong enough and deep enough, we can be free from pain is most often based on fear. We fear, perhaps more than anything, the helplessness of the loss of control. For some, like myself, our reaction may be to cling to identities—of the doer who can accomplish things, of the knower who can control life through knowing—that we hope will ward off our experiencing the fear of helplessness. This fear of helplessness also prevents us from experiencing genuine compassion. It is so much easier to write someone off (including ourselves) by reducing illness to some blind spot that is not being faced than it is to feel the helplessness and loss of control that illness often triggers. But the real key is to surrender to helplessness itself. We can do this only when we give up asking why (again, the mind hoping to control through "knowing") and instead simply attend to the "what" of the moment. This "what" is not just the physical discomfort but all the deeply held beliefs associated with the discomfort. We get so hooked into trying to find the meaning behind our illness or pain that we often ignore the incredible teachings that are right there in front of us—within the whatness of our present-moment experience of symptoms/beliefs/emotions.

An old Zen line says, "On a withered tree, a flower blooms." We often think that being healed means the illness and pain will go away. But healing does not necessarily mean that the physical body will mend, any more than a withered tree will become young again. Healing is not just about physical symptoms. Many people heal and still remain physically sick or even die. Many who become physically well never really heal. Healing involves clearing the pathway to the open heart—the heart that knows only connectedness. When we experience this openness, the flower blooms regardless of what happens to our body. In *The Diving Bell and the Butterfly*, the author—though completely immobilized and subjected to endless discomforts—was still able, at least in some measure, to fly free as a butterfly. To heal, to become whole, means we no longer identify with ourselves as just this body, as just our suffering. We identify with a vaster sense of being.

The fact is that the heart is always open. However, the pathway to this heart is blocked by years of conditioning. It is overgrown with protections, pretenses, deeply held core beliefs, pictures of who we think we should be, fears, anger, confusion, and our resistance to life as it is. Mostly we don't want our pain or our suffering. Mostly we want to be taken care of. We want someone (such as a mate or a teacher) or something (such as more favorable life circumstances or a big experience) to make everything OK. But until we're willing to learn from our suffering, the path to the open heart will stay blocked. Until we stop running away from our pain, our suffering will continue. Perhaps the greatest pain is our resistance to pain itself.

But sometimes we can't run away. Sometimes very difficult circumstances in life make it clear that there's no easy way out. Who's to say how difficult things have to get before we stop resisting? Who's to say how long it will take to learn what it means to become willing? At what point will we be able to recognize that the painful circumstances of our life really are our best teacher? When I reflect back on this period of my life when I felt most lost, I can see clearly that it was the illness, and all the baggage that came along with it—namely, all "my suffering"—that was the catalyst to turn my life right-side up.

I didn't want my nausea or my illness; I didn't want my sense of loss. I just wanted them to disappear. Thus "my suffering" arose. Once I understood that my illness was my path, it gradually became clear that real healing was not about the body's getting better or about having all the suffering disappear. It was about being willing to let all of it just be. It was about bringing awareness to the layers of emotion-based beliefs that were blocking access to the open heart. Of course, I still cared about recovering physically. I continue to do whatever seems helpful for bringing my body into balance, including seeking tradition- al medical care, as well as enjoyments such as eating chocolate or outings to the movies. But what I've truly discovered is an inner understanding that no longer denies the value of pain, dif- ficult circumstances, and suffering.

Once I got over the worst of the physical symptoms and began to function fairly well, I realized how easy it would be to slip back into old routines. I could use the remission of my immune system disease to pretend that everything was fine. But fortunately I had learned enough to know that this would just be more skating on thin ice. I began the practice of desig- nating one day a week as a "sick day." No matter how well I was feeling, I would live that day as if I were still sick. Although I would not spend hours on the couch as I had during some phases of the illness, I would intentionally slow down all my movements. I could then appreciate the depths of aware- ness that are possible when we slow down enough to let life in: observing thoughts without getting caught in them, feeling the texture of life without resisting, seeing how we don't need to be so busy, dropping attachment to comfort, seeing into the roots of fear, experiencing the quiet joy of mundane activities. I so value this one-day practice for keeping my priorities straight that I have continued it over the last nine years.

As well, I became a hospice volunteer. My job is to go to the homes of terminally ill patients, to simply be with them or help them in any way I can. This "practice" has been invaluable to me, in that the intensity of the situation helps keep me at my edge. Seeing others in pain, seeing others struggling with the often intense suffering surrounding death, serves to bring what- ever unhealed pain remains back to the surface. But now I can experience this with the understanding that pain simply is and that when we resist it, when we believe the thoughts that arise out of it, we turn our pain into the heaviness of "my suffering."

Each hospice visit reminds me that what is required for real healing is that instead of pushing away our pain, we acknowledge it, experience its texture as best we can, and allow it to penetrate to the open heart. This kind of healing does not come from forced effort, nor from doing battle with ourselves. It comes from a soft effort born of the understanding that there is no enemy. As this understanding deepens, as we become more willing to allow life to just be, we discover one essential ingredient in the process: kindness.

Although I have been basically healthy for the last several years, occasionally the old symptoms reappear full-blown and intense, lasting from several hours to several days. Sometimes, when I'm reduced to lying in a fetal position, I watch, on an almost microscopic level, how I try to turn this pain into suffering. Thoughts of resistance flood my mind, followed by the voices of fear and self-pity. As soon as I hear these voices for what they are, they lose their hold. My awareness goes directly to the center of the chest—breathing into the heartspace on the inbreath and extending loving-kindness to my body on the outbreath.

Although I believe that awareness is instrumental in bringing the body back into balance, who is to say how these processes really work? One thing I can say with certainty is that as long as we resist our pain, as long as we see our difficulties as obstacles, as long as we continue to struggle against ourselves, we can never really heal. We will remain forever locked inside our own diving bell of suffering.

Working with our pain and suffering requires both the precision of seeing clearly through our believed thoughts and a softening awareness that allows us to enter with a light touch into those areas we have tended to avoid. Working in this way, we see how much of our suffering is unnecessary. This clarity, in turn, gives us the courage to continue working with suffering, even through those moments when it seems as if it will never end. What arises is an increasing compassion for both ourselves and the whole human drama. We see that pain and suffering are not the endgame; they are simply the most effective vehicles for awakening our hearts.

11

Practicing with Distress

THE FEELING THAT LIFE is out of sync and that there is too much to do is not new. As Buddha pointed out more than twenty-six hundred years ago, we'll always have to deal with pain and suffering. We will always have our "eighty-three problems"—concerns about financial security, difficulties in relationships, fears about our health, anxious striving toward success and acceptance, and so on. Perhaps it's the "eighty-fourth problem"—that we don't really want to have any problems—that makes our current time seem so full of distress.

Many people come to meditation practice with the expectation that it will calm them and relieve their stress. Certainly meditation can do this to some extent; even the most superficial meditation practices can induce feelings of calmness. And the more comprehensive forms of meditation can move us well beyond superficial calmness into a wider container of awareness. Within this more spacious context, we can experience daily ups and downs with equanimity.

However, when we're knee-deep in emotional distress, we're fortunate if we can remember to practice at all. When caught in the middle of swirling thoughts and rampant emotions, how can we really practice? We can't just remove ourselves from the difficult situation and go off to meditate. Even if we could, sitting down to follow the breath is unlikely to bring peace of mind at times when we are using emotional reactivity as a Band-Aid to cover our deeper difficulties.

When the clarity of practice becomes obscured by the dark and swirling energy of emotional distress, it is useful to have some clear and concise reminders to bring us back to reality. We need to learn how, specifically, we can effectively practice when caught in our own mess. Although practice can never be reduced to a formula or a collection of techniques, there are certain guidelines that can be useful for practicing with difficult emotional reactions, especially our most deep-seated reactions—those that arise directly from our core fears and pain. The following four reminders embody the understanding that will help us when we feel most lost.

The first reminder is to *awaken aspiration*. On an elementary level, to awaken aspiration means simply that we remember to practice. Once we remember to practice, to awaken aspiration means that we see our particular distress *as our path*. Instead of seeing our distress as the enemy, as something to get rid of; instead of giving it juice by solidifying the thoughts around it into the heaviness and drama of "me," we learn to view distress as our opportunity to see and to open. We relate to it as our path to awakening.

When we find ourselves in a mess, we might have the thought, "This isn't how life is supposed to be." Our present discomfort doesn't conform to our picture of how life should unfold. When life doesn't fit our picture, we usually feel that something is wrong. But it is not so much that something is wrong as it is that we're relating to life from the narrow, fear-based perspective of "I want." What we want is to feel good, and when our emotional distress does not feel good, we almost instinctively move away from it. Our discomfort generates fear, and in that fear there is even more discomfort. No wonder we tend to see distress as the enemy, as something to get rid of.

We have to turn our upside-down view right-side up to understand what it means to see difficulties as our path. When I first understood this teaching experientially—not just as a good intellectual insight—I felt my relationship to life shift 180 degrees. The main issue was no longer just about whether I felt good or whether I liked what was happening. The main issue was to be more awake, to learn what I had to learn to stop holding back my heart in fear. This didn't mean that I had to like what was on my plate; what it meant was that the willingness to open to life's difficulties does not depend on *having* to like them. Seeing our difficulties as our path, allowing them to awaken our aspiration, means that we are willing to let them in, regardless of how we may be feeling. It means that our main priority is to learn, to open, to awaken.

The second reminder is to *awaken curiosity*, asking the practice question "What *is* this?" This is not an expression of idle curiosity, nor is it an analytical exploration. It's awakening the desire to know the truth of the moment through experiencing. We cannot know the truth of the moment through experiencing as long as we're blaming, wallowing in "poor me," trying to escape, or giving credence to powerful thoughts such as "This isn't fair" and "I can't do this." The thought realm is where we stay stuck; it's where things become solid, dark, and unworkable. In awakening curiosity, we return over and over again to the bodily experience of the moment, to the physical "whatness" of our experience, which is movable, light, and workable.

Several years ago I was faced with an alarming reading on a screening test for prostate cancer. Instead of having a biopsy, I chose to treat myself with a combination of healing meditation, acupuncture, and herbs for six months. Then I took another test to see to what extent the cancer cells remained, if at all. Aware that it would be very unpleasant to have my prostate removed and that I might then be incontinent and impotent, I felt a great deal of fear while waiting for the results. I practiced staying with the body, asking over and over, "What *is* this?" The combination of fear and self-pity was powerful, as was the desire to escape, but my continuous effort to return to the physical reality of the moment began to undercut the solidity of my fear. The question "What is this?" worked like a laser in focusing on the experience of fear itself. After two days of practice, I realized that none of what I feared was happening now, nor had it ever happened! There was no real pain other than that generated by my thoughts. This realization effectively burst the bubble of my fears. The insight did not come from thinking but from staying with the "whatness" of the moment. It came from being curious about reality.

The third reminder in working with distress is to *awaken humor*, or at least some wider perspective. Anytime we're obsessing over something that's happening mainly in our thoughts, it is helpful to remember Mark Twain's words: "I'm a very old man. I've had lots of problems. Most of them never happened."

One way to broaden our perspective is to see the difficulties as just another aspect of our conditioning playing itself out. When we remember this, we can say to ourselves, "Here it comes again. What will it be like this time?" This is not a trick to avoid facing our issues; rather, it is a means of getting just enough perspective to be able to enter into the difficulty without being overwhelmed by it. We can also ask ourselves, "Have I ever had this problem before?" Of course, we have— probably over and over. Can we see it for what it is, just our conditioning? Looking at a difficulty like this breaks our iden- tification with it; it provides some spaciousness, a bigger context; it broadens the narrow tunnel vision that often ac- companies distress.

Once when my Pandora's box was opening wide, I went to Joko to describe what was happening. I felt dark and grim and was embarrassed to reveal that I was experiencing so much fear. She smiled at me and said, "That's pretty interesting. Let's look at this." I got the sense that it wasn't me we were talking about but just "stuff." Here was a wider perspective. It's not that the fears were an illusion and could therefore be ignored, but that they were simply my particular conditioning. Putting them in this context allowed me to look more lightly at "my fears." I even saw the humor in the fact that my father, in repeatedly quoting to me the line "There's nothing to fear but fear itself," had succeeded in convincing me that I should be afraid of fear—quite the opposite of his benign intention. Cultivating humor and a larger perspective was instrumental in helping me to emerge from what had been a lifelong tunnel of fear.

Since then I've developed an exercise, which I practice on occasion, usually for a whole day. Every time I find myself caught in a reaction or a judgment, especially about myself, I become aware on the inbreath and say the words "not me." It helps me see my reactions and judgments as just conditioning. Then I use the outbreath to soften the edges around my suffering.

Unlike a positive affirmation, this exercise is not a cosmetic overlay. It requires that we still see our thoughts clearly, with precision. To do it, we still need to reside in the physical aspect of our experience. But it lightens the myopic and self-centered perspective that often accompanies the process of learning to know ourselves. In the process it serves as a reminder of the bigger view and helps generate compassion.

Much of the heaviness of our distress comes from the belief that we should be different. Especially after practicing for a few years, we think we shouldn't still be so reactive. We think we should be beyond our conditioning. But practice doesn't work that way. A more accurate view of what happens in practice is that at first we have a willful Great Dane on a leash who pulls us along whenever and wherever it wants to go. After many years we still feel the tug on the leash, and we still hear the dog yapping to go. Our conditioning is still there. But when we look at the dog, we see that it's just a Chihuahua now. To work with it, all we have to do is let it yap as it will and jerk the leash lightly.

The fourth reminder is to awaken *loving-kindness*. This is the ability to bring nonjudgmental awareness from the heart to the unwanted aspects of "me." This reminder can't be overemphasized. It's so natural to want to confirm what is most negative about ourselves that we don't even think about activating compassion or kindness. Yet when we soften our self-judgment with loving-kindness, the sense of drama and heaviness lightens considerably.

For example, when confusion arises, instead of condemning ourselves, we acknowledge and experience what's happening, learning to extend compassionate awareness to this confused being called "me." When illness arises, instead of seeing ourselves as defective or analyzing why we are ill, we can come from the heart to extend loving-kindness awareness into this physical body. The effect can be an increased sense of softening and spaciousness. As we practice awakening loving-kindness regularly, it becomes more and more a part of our being, our natural response to life.

Sometimes when emotional distress is particularly powerful, nothing we've learned about practicing with distress seems relevant. Dense and intense emotional reactions can leave us feeling lost and overwhelmed. In these darkest moments, the practice is to bring awareness to the center of the chest, breathing the painful emotions, via the inbreath, directly into the heartspace. It's as if we were breathing the swirling physical sensations right into the heart. Then, on the outbreath, we simply exhale. We're not trying to do or change anything; we're simply allowing our heart center to become a wider container of awareness within which to experience distress.

It's when we become lost in these darkest emotions that we're likely to judge ourselves most harshly. We solidify our negative core beliefs that we are unworthy, weak, and hopeless. There seems to be no way out of our shame. Breathing the painful sensations right into the heartspace undercuts the power of these deeply held core beliefs. Breathing into the heart is an act of compassion; by opening to our negative self-judgment in this way, we are opening to the universal pain of being human.

This practice takes us to the edge, the point beyond which

we think we can't go. Breathing into the center of the chest, taking that one breath directly into the heartspace, opening to the pain that feels as if it's going to do us in, teaches us that it won't do us in. We begin to experience the spaciousness of the heart, where our hard-hearted judgments soften and our darkest moods lighten up. We begin to understand that awareness heals; and to open to this healing, one more breath into the heart is all that's required.

The four basic reminders for practicing with emotional distress are:

1. *Awakening aspiration*: seeing our distress as the path to awakening
2. *Awakening curiosity*: experiencing the physical reality of the moment by asking "What *is* it?"
3. *Awakening humor*: seeing our difficulties from an enlarged perspective as simply the "stuff" of our conditioning
4. *Awakening loving-kindness*: allowing the spaciousness of the open heart to heal our deepest shame and darkest states of mind

Working with these four reminders entails revisiting some fundamental practice questions: "What are the thoughts?" "What are my pictures, my requirements here?" "How do I think it's 'supposed' to be?" We have to label our thoughts again and again to clearly see all the ideals and expectations out of which we live. And along with uncovering our deep beliefs, we must repeatedly return to residing in the physical reality of the moment.

To willingly reside in our distress, no longer resisting what is, is the real key to transformation. This means learning to welcome our difficulties. What does it mean to welcome a difficulty? It's not that we seek out our deep fears, humiliation, or longing, but that, when we meet them, we open fully to their searing power. To find the way to the open heart, we must work with whatever blocks the path. As painful as it may be to face our deepest fears, we do reach the point at which it's more painful not to face them. This is a pivotal point in the practice life.

In the movie *Say Anything*, a high school senior wants to ask the most beautiful, intelligent girl in the class out on a date. After listening to his friends' repeated admonishments that he is a "nerd" who is just going to be hurt, he flings his arms out wide and shouts, "I *want* to be hurt!" He understands that to be truly open, he has to risk being vulnerable.

In the midst of our drama, it's sometimes helpful to consciously remember how it's keeping us from living our genuine life. Feeling the limitation of our fears, shame, and suffering and breathing it into the heartspace allows us to penetrate the protective barriers that comprise our substitute way of being. As we begin to move beyond the artificial construct that we call a "self"—the seat of all our emotional distress— we enter into a wider container of awareness. We see that our emotional drama, however distressful, is still just thoughts, just memories, just sensations. Who we really are—our basic connectedness—is so much bigger than just this body, just this personal drama.

Seeing this bigger picture one time, two times, or even a dozen times doesn't mean we'll no longer have emotional reactions. But keeping the bigger picture in view does help us avoid getting lost in our distress as quickly, as intensely, or for as long. We begin to understand and even believe that all our stuff is workable. We can finally know that no matter how messy or painful our emotional state may be, it's still, at bottom, just deeply held thoughts combined with strong or uncomfortable physical sensations. All that's required of us is the willingness to be with what is. When we finally allow ourselves to be with what we'd rather avoid—which is simply not feeling good— then our very drama becomes the path to freedom.

12

Work and Practice

DURING MY MIDTWENTIES I worked in traditional white-col-
lar jobs, first as a teacher and then as a computer programmer.
But I was not happy. I hated what I was doing and anguished for
more than a year over finding my "real lifework." I was just
beginning to practice, and a fellow practitioner suggested that
every time anxiety arose over what kind of work would be right
for me, I refrain from thinking about it and instead attempt to
feel the physical reality of my life in that moment. At the time
his approach made no sense to me, but I was desperate enough
to try it anyway. After practicing this way for a few months,
even though I didn't get any insights into what work to pursue,
I sensed something genuine about the quality of awareness that
was apparent when I put thinking aside and focused on the
"whatness" of the moment. Then one day, almost out of the
blue, I realized that "my path" was to become a carpenter. Even
though I had no experience in carpentry, it was clear that in
learning to be a carpenter, I would have to address many of the
fears and self-beliefs that I knew were holding me back.

In trying to make an important decision such as what direction our work should take, it helps to be willing to drop the
endless weighing and measuring of pros and cons. The spinning mind will just continue to spin. The genuine answers can
only come from having a clear understanding of who we are
and what our life is. But this type of understanding will be
clouded until we drop our mental obsessing and enter into the

physical experience of the anguish of not knowing what to do. As the light of awareness penetrates through the layers of tension and dis-ease, we encounter a clarity of purpose that would forever elude us if we worked solely on trying to unravel our mental world.

The attachment to figuring out our decisions through thinking is based on the all-too-human tendency to seek ground beneath our feet. When contemplating what our lifework might be, our attachment to security and a sense of safety is what drives us. We gravitate toward thinking in the belief that we can avoid experiencing the sense of groundlessness inherent in change. But entering into groundlessness itself is the key to resolving our problem. Our willingness to experience the physical sense of no ground is what will eventually bring us to clarity, because it will allow us to see through the roots of our fear. But we can do this only when we're finally willing to give up our addiction to subjective thinking. I'm not suggesting that we throw all our thinking aside. There will always be practical considerations—money, education, and so on—but these logistical factors cannot be our main focus in settling on what our work will be.

Perhaps the one question that we don't ask often enough is "What do I have to offer?" We are so intent on analyzing what we can get from a job or an occupation that we rarely consider the sense of satisfaction that comes from offering our unique contribution. We could take the question "What do I have to offer?" as a koan, leaving the world of mental analysis in order to enter into the experience of not knowing. Simply raising the question and focusing on the gestalt of the moment may not bring any immediate answers. Nor is it particularly pleasant, since it brings us once again face-to-face with the experience of no ground. However, there is something about being in the moment that is compelling, real, and far removed from the confused spinning of the mental world.

• • •

A more common difficulty that arises around work is finding ourselves in a situation in which we feel stuck, anxious, or simply unhappy. We don't necessarily want a different occupation, but we constantly question whether to change jobs. In the context of practice, this is an interesting question. Our conventional response to an uncomfortable job situation is to believe that something is wrong and look for a way out. But in the practice life, we don't measure the value of something by how much pleasure or comfort it brings. We do, however, recognize the value of distress, in that what we learn from our distress can transform us. We know through practice that just because something requires an effort that feels uncomfortable doesn't necessarily make it undesirable. That a situation feels bad doesn't make it bad. From a practice perspective, the case is often just the opposite.

If you're having a strong emotional reaction to your job, it's a given that from the practice point of view, there is something of value to be learned. The problem is not simply the job. Of two people doing the same job, one may feel satisfaction while the other feels nothing but distress. Our emotional reaction is primarily based on what *we* bring to the job rather than the job itself. Our reactions are always tied to the baggage we bring in—expectations, needs, and agendas.

It's not that we should stay in a job just in order to practice. But we should at least consider what we can learn from a job before we decide to leave. It's helpful to remain in a job as long as you're having strong emotional reactions, in order to see through your believed thoughts and conditioned fears. Because one thing is certain: if you leave to go to another job, you will take the same beliefs and fears with you. If staying in a particular job is unrealistic, you can set a time limit on how long you'll stay, aspiring to learn as much as you can within that time limit.

Even if we like our work, or at least have no intention of leaving our present job, there are always ways in which we can make awareness practice a greater part of our workday. Perhaps more than anything, this requires a shift from how we normally relate to our work—as separate from practice—to seeing our work as our path. We often forget what our real job—our life job—is. Our life job is to become awake to who we really are. When we remember this, we will be less likely to separate our work from our practice. We'll begin to understand that it's possible to practice with *everything* we encounter, even at work. To make this shift challenges our long-standing conditioned views and habits; consequently the best way to transform the relationship with our workday is by taking small steps. This is where mindfulness practice, in which we bring attention to the texture of the present moment, can be particularly helpful.

Applying mindfulness is the blue-collar work of practice. There is nothing romantic, mystical, or even exciting about dealing with the nuts and bolts of our mundane daily routine, beyond the subtle satisfaction that comes with beginning to understand that it's possible to practice with everything. We see that picking up a ringing phone, closing a door, becoming aware of sounds, or even going to the bathroom can all be used as reminders to be awake in the moment. Our work then becomes an opportunity to wake up.

One of the keys in practicing with work entails looking at the emotional dramas that keep repeating themselves in the work environment. Whatever core beliefs we've developed, whatever our particular behavioral strategies are, they're sure to muck things up at work as much as they do in our relationships. The less personalized environment of work can be helpful in reflecting back to us the patterns we're repeating in every other aspect of our lives.

Beginning when I was eleven, I worked for my father during the summer for ten years. My brother and sisters and I were the sales force for his souvenir store on the boardwalk in Atlantic City. Although we were pretty aggressive salespeople, when my father perceived that business was not going well, he would sometimes explode in anger. Unfortunately the anger was usually directed at one of his children; most often, it seemed, at me. My father was quite powerful when he was angry. He would shout about how I wasn't trying, how I was unappreciative, how I was just going through the motions. When he'd shout like this, everyone in the store would freeze. Then, when he stomped out of the store, the nervous customers, especially the customers I was waiting on, would start buying like crazy. Looking back, this seems almost comical, but at the time good humor was far from my mind.

As angry as I'd get when I felt I'd been unjustifiably picked on, I was nonetheless your typical good boy and would proceed to try harder. At one point I started listing all my sales and adding them up at the end of the day. I'd show this list to my father to prove to him that I was measuring up. For many years, in a variety of contexts, I continued this strategy of "making a list" to prove that I was worthy. I felt that if I could tangibly demonstrate my success, my productivity, my value, it would ward off the core fear of being judged unworthy.

Of course, this strategy, like all strategies of behavior modification, never really worked. Perhaps it allowed me to achieve external success in that it drove me to excel, but it never addressed my core fear that I was not measuring up. The core fear, and all the day-to-day anxiety that arose out of it, could only be held at bay temporarily. As long as we don't see clearly that we are just acting from pictures, and as long as we don't open up to experiencing the layers of protection and fear that underlie most of these pictures, any meaningful transformation will elude us. When I finally started seeing this dynamic for what it was, I was able to approach my deeply ingrained behavior pattern quite differently. Instead of trying to live out of the picture that I had to measure up, instead of following the behavior of "making my lists," I learned to bring awareness to the fear itself.

Each of us has to see our own version of "making a list." Is your style to get hooked into the "child" identity, needing to please and get approval from someone whom you blindly identify as an authority? Or is your pattern to be busy, busy, busy, with the anxious feeling that you're trying to juggle at least one too many plates? Can you see the addictive quality of the busyness, how you use it to validate your own worth, to distract yourself from the underlying fear of being "nothing"? Although we believe that we have to do everything on our plate, all it takes is a prolonged bout of illness to show us that this is not true. We are not indispensable, and much of what we think we have to do can be delegated, put on hold, or even deleted from our agenda. The problem is not how much work we have to do but how we're using that work to bolster and solidify our identity. Living the practice life is about becoming free of *any* restricting identity, especially those based primarily in fear.

Perhaps your personal system is based more in worry, whether over job performance, job security, or financial insecurities. Whatever the content of the worries, the real issue is the addiction to worry itself; more to the point, it's the addiction to maintaining the *self*. In all these examples, the practice is the same. First, we have to see clearly our specific habitual patterns. Second, we have to see the pictures and beliefs from which we're living. And third, we have to let ourselves experience the fears out of which all these beliefs and behaviors arise. When we start using our work environment in this way—using our emotional upheavals to help us dismantle our self-identity (who we think we are)—we can move from being caught in the chaos of the workplace to using that same chaos as our vehicle to become free.

There is also the issue of burnout. In burnout not only have we lost our motivation to work, but we've also become cynical and negative about ever finding satisfaction in what we're doing. In living the practice life, the first step in dealing with burnout is an increased awareness of what *we've* brought to the job. In other words, instead of focusing on the shortcomings of our job situation or the people we work with, we look at ourselves. For example, we can firmly believe that "I can't do the kind of job that I was trained for" or "I'm just going through the motions." These thoughts may even be true. However, a strong emotional reaction to our situation—be it frustration, anger, or cynicism—is a clear indicator that we need to move away from blame and focus on what we ourselves have brought to the job. What are our expectations and requirements? Where are we attached to the results of our actions? Where do we think we can control results, make things right, change people? Seeing ourselves as the one who can get things done or becoming attached to the results of what we do will surely lead to the frustration and disappointment of burnout, because we simply can't legislate how things will turn out.

In the meantime we're missing the key issue: our attachment to results is almost always based on the need to bolster a particular self-image or to avoid experiencing the fear of failure or the fear of being no one. Sooner or later we will have to deal with the groundlessness that comes when our false sense of security is challenged or removed. Sooner or later we'll have to go to the roots of the fears and beliefs that tell us, in one way or another, that we're not quite good enough and never will be.

Practicing with burnout means we have to come to know our motives, our expectations, our agendas—all the basic belief systems that run our lives. It requires us to wake up to all our restricting pictures and identities. It also requires that we learn to face and experience the fears that have been running us. But facing these fears need not be a dark or grim task. Within the wider container of awareness practice, we can experience these fears with an increasing sense of lightness and spaciousness. We can learn that burnout, like all our endless suffering, is always optional. From a practice perspective, nothing could be more fertile than burnout.

I don't mean to imply that all the difficulties we encounter at work are self-induced. There are certainly real challenges that have to be addressed. But our emotional reactions to these challenges are our own. Furthermore, when we stay stuck in our reactions, we are less able to deal clearly with the real challenges of our work. As long as we are attached to achieving a particular result or to being seen in a particular way, that attachment will obstruct our ability to do our job wholeheartedly. It will also get in the way of experiencing the satisfaction that is possible when we simply do our best. The more we can bring practice to our work, and thereby see through our requirements of how things should be, the more we will be able to live in a genuine way, free from the compulsions of mindlessness and fear.

PART III

awakening the heart
of compassion

13
Hard and Soft

THE STORY OF THE ZEN MONK who cuts off his arm to prove his determination to practice and the image of the Buddha's inscrutable smile point to a delicate interplay in living the practice life. On the one hand, we make disciplined efforts, and on the other hand, we just let be. Often we get confused by this distinction; and because we are prone to black-or-white thinking, we imagine that practice must be one way or the other. Either we see how important discipline is and exert strong effort, or we realize the necessity to refrain from grasping, from trying to get somewhere special, and consequently soften our approach, just letting things be.

For example, the essence of sitting meditation is simply to be here, to bring full awareness to this very moment. But what actually goes on is the incessant outpouring of our overactive brain—planning, fantasizing, conversing, worrying, and so on. In order not to get hooked by each passing thought, we learn the discipline of coming back again and again, moment after moment, to awareness of the breath, the body, the environment. We also learn the disciplined precision of labeling our thoughts, so we can know with clarity what we're thinking while simultaneously breaking the identification with our thoughts. As we see them more and more clearly as just thoughts, we believe in them less and less as "the Truth."

Discipline, or hard effort, is also necessary to stay with practice through all the inevitable ups and downs. At every moment we have a choice: to live the practice life or go for what makes us feel comfortable and secure. In practice we learn the value of making the effort to turn away from comfort or predictability, even when we would like nothing more than to give up on this seemingly hopeless effort to awaken.

Discipline is so important that it's easy to get lost in a picture of practice as some stoic, almost militant enterprise. At times we hold the belief that unless we maintain our discipline, we will fall apart; we might even lose our identity as a serious and spiritual person. So we continue to struggle against those parts of ourselves that we think will undermine our practice. Yet in buckling down, we fall into the pattern of relentless self-judgment, of believing thoughts about how practice should be, about how *I* should be.

Then perhaps we get some insight into what we're doing and move to the other end of the continuum. We remember the teaching that everything is fine just as it is; that within the passing show there is nothing to do, nowhere to go, no one to be. So we drop the discipline and try to relax into what is. We try to just let things be. But in trying to soften, we are going as much off course as in being militant in our effort. Just because everything is in fact fine just as it is does not necessarily mean that we *experience* everything as fine just as it is. To pretend that we do is a cosmetic overlay. It bypasses the necessity of putting effort into the task of clarifying our own messy life.

The interplay between hard and soft is the essence of practice. Without learning what it means to interweave the hard and the soft, we restrict our practice in such a way that it is never complete or satisfying, because it narrows the flow of our natural being to just one stream.

The interplay between hard and soft is difficult to explain. We need to experience it in order to understand what it is. It boils down to learning that *within* the discipline of choosing to be here at each moment, we realize that whenever we do spin off, especially into areas of ourselves that we don't like—confusion, anxiety, discouragement—we can foster a sense of spaciousness, compassion, and kindness toward the whole struggle. Instead of being caught in a narrow and dark tunnel vision of who we think we are, with all its heaviness and seriousness, we learn what it means to see our "stuff" as simply conditioning, as just ancient wounds and core beliefs.

When we find ourselves spinning off into the mental realm, our usual pattern is to heap on layers of believed judgment and self-judgment: "This is too difficult," "I can't do this," "I'm hopeless." These layers only thicken the callous shell around the heart. Cultivating a sense of space allows us to stop the "hard" approach of struggling against ourselves by pushing away our stuff as bad or as an illusion. Softening allows our inherent compassion and kindness to emerge, which, in turn, allows us to be with whatever arises. It doesn't mean that we like it, but that we can relate to it in a new way.

Our drama, pain, and suffering sometimes feel like death itself. One of the lessons of the practice life is that this heaviness is really no more than a combination of deeply believed thoughts and fairly intense physical sensations. This *experiential* understanding is what gives us the spaciousness to let our pain just be there, as unpleasant as it may be. We still need to work with it; we can't just label it as empty and pretend to let it go. That wouldn't be genuine. But we can learn to approach it with a certain lightness of heart. Learning to do this is what transforms and softens our *will*—as ego, as striving, as struggle—into *willingness*.

Take the example of sitting with pain. What type of effort do we need to work with physical pain when the ankles hurt, the knees hurt, the back hurts, or we ache all over? Maybe it is necessary sometimes to grit our way through with a hard effort. But we can also gradually learn about the soft effort of just being here with the body, no longer feeling identified as just a body or just the pain. As we use hard effort—discipline and precision—to stop believing in the thoughts "This is too painful" and "I can't take this anymore," our humorless self-centered identifications lighten up. This doesn't mean we like the pain; it simply means we stop struggling against the pain and against ourselves. We learn that we can even willingly be here with the unpleasant sensations. What evolves in the process of seeing through our believed thoughts is a receptivity to what is. This is the soft effort.

This process of interweaving hard and soft effort is particularly important in working with addictions. Of course, the first stage in working with an addiction is to become aware of the addictive behavior and also of the extent to which we are being run by the addictive urges. The main effort in this stage is to apply clarity and precision of awareness to what is actually going on. It is here that the discipline of self-observation is key. How else will we see the aspects of ourselves that we would prefer to ignore or deny? As long as we don't acknowledge our addictions for what they are, we can't work with them.

Once we are clear about what is going on, the second stage in working with addictions is to try to refrain from the addictive behavior. This type of discipline is what we are calling a hard effort, but soft effort also is necessary. The soft effort is what will keep us from getting lost in the tunnel vision of negative self-judgment. When we struggle with addiction, it's almost certain that we will buy into the belief that our addiction is bad or that we're bad because we have it. This grafted-on layer of heaviness and gloom makes our attempts to refrain from the addictive behavior even more difficult than they already are. For the discipline to be effective, we must soften the harshness of our self-judgment.

The third stage in working with addictions is to experience the urges out of which our addictive behaviors arise. This requires the hard effort of *What is it?* mind, in which we focus the laser beam of awareness on the physical reality of the moment. Once we experience the addictive urge, we can enlist the softer quality and just let it be. It can be particularly helpful to feel the quality of the craving on the inbreath. There's something about experiencing our cravings on the inbreath that allows them to soften.

The last stage of working with addictions is to experience the suppressed pain under the addictive urge. Again, this requires the hard effort of *What is it?* mind as well as the softer effort of just letting the feelings be, without getting caught in self-judgments. At this stage it is very important to be able to bring a sense of space and kindness to practice. Otherwise, we continue in the potentially endless struggle against ourselves, in which it is so easy to sink into believed thoughts of shame, self-hatred, and hopelessness. In remembering to bring an artful, light-hearted touch to the struggle, we can balance our efforts in such a way that even our most entrenched patterns seem workable. Even in our most claustrophobic moments, all we have to do is take a few breaths into the heartspace to discover a spaciousness big enough to include everything—our most seemingly solid fears and our harshest self-judgments. Of course, we need to practice with each of these stages over and over.

Here is another example of soft effort. When my immune system disorder flares up, I feel very weak and nauseous. Even though most of the time it's relatively OK, sometimes it comes on so intensely and fast that my first response—despite years of practicing with it—is to want it to just go away.

During a particularly strong flare-up, when I was lying in bed in the middle of the night with unrelenting nausea, I saw myself relating to the symptoms almost as the enemy. But from labeling the fear-based thoughts and being able to see through them, something clicked, and I realized the depth of my misunderstanding. Although I can try to push away my experience, the fact remains that whatever is happening right now is my genuine life. Like it or not, want it or not, this life is what is. To embrace it rather than push it away is the key to freedom. Understanding this allowed me to experience, once again, what it means to soften into the whole struggle, to cease resistance to what is. With this understanding I became willing to affirm that I was on board. Regardless of whether I liked the trip, I would take the ride to see what it was like and where it was going, without the extra baggage of self-pity and fear. Self-pity, fear, the complaints—all the judgments—are the real obstacles to softening and surrendering to what is.

This is the natural progression of the practice life. We need the discipline to see these layers of judgmental thoughts and mental pictures. And it requires hard effort to stay with the bodily discomfort that comes with these thoughts. Yet we also need to understand how simply breathing into the center of the chest, residing in the quiver of being, and then extending spaciousness and compassion to our struggling, conditioned patterns is the essence of what it means to soften. To soften difficult self-beliefs is to truly understand that these are not the deepest truths about ourselves. As we learn how to make this soft effort around our relentlessly judging mind, as we learn what it means to awaken a sense of heart, we begin to relate in a new, more spacious way to the ancient wound of our seeming separateness. What we're doing is learning to receive and accept the whole of our being, just as it is, no longer judging, editing, rejecting.

Through the disciplined precision of our efforts, we'll come again and again to our edge—the difficult places beyond which we've previously been unable to move. Through the willingness to soften and surrender to what is, we learn that we can gradually move beyond that edge. It is only through this interplay of hard and soft, of effort and letting be, of will and willingness, that we learn to our amazement that we can emerge from the lifelong tunnel of fear that constitutes our substitute life into the nitty-gritty reality of our genuine one.

14
Letting Be

THE POWER OF OUR CULTURAL CONDITIONING became clear
to me recently when I was told about a man and his son who
were in an automobile accident. The man died, and the boy was
brought to the hospital. The surgeon, upon entering the operating room, said, "I can't operate on this boy. He's my son."

The person who told this story asked me, "Who's the surgeon?" At first I thought the whole thing was a Zen koan. I had
no idea how to respond. But the answer was simple: the surgeon was the boy's mother. This most obvious answer didn't
even occur to me. Although I don't think I am consciously
biased against women, the strength of our cultural conditioning was apparent in my assumption that the surgeon was a
man. This drove home the point that many of our actions are
based on culturally conditioned perceptions about which we
may not be the least bit aware. How much of what we do is the
result of this mostly unseen conditioning?

In the practice life, there is one particular cultural attitude
that may wreak more havoc than any other: the deeply seated
view that we have to *do*. We are culturally conditioned to
believe that it is good to be active, to be productive. We have
been programmed to assume that the way to happiness is to follow our inner compulsion to change and fix ourselves. The
sense that we can *do* something to make things better is a
deeply ingrained quality of our substitute life.

The basic theme of sitting practice—no matter what we

bring in the door or how we may be feeling—is simply to sit and let it be. We sit down, become aware of what's happening in our bodies and minds, experience its texture, and then just let it be.

We can use the practice question "What's going on right now?" to become aware of the state of our mind, the state of our body, and the sensory input from the environment. To experience this, ask yourself this question right now. What is going on in this very moment? Notice your state of mind. Is it busy? Confused? Calm? Upset? Just notice. Also, notice the state of your body. Is it tired? Relaxed? Achy? Settled? Again, just be aware. Now notice the input from the environment— the temperature in the room, the shades of light, the sounds. You don't have to do anything—just become aware of it.

As we become aware of the textures of the moment, we're rarely willing to experience them the way they are. We're apt to see one aspect or another as a problem to be solved or an obstacle to be overcome. This is because we believe in our judgements and opinions about whatever is going on. For example, if we're bored or sleepy during sitting, we usually judge it as a bad sitting. If we feel agitated or upset, we think we have to calm down. When we feel confused, we may long for clarity. But our practice is to simply remember that no matter what may be happening, it need not be seen as an obstacle or enemy, nor as something to fix or change or get rid of. From a practice point of view, whatever it is, it's our path.

We only need to ask the question "What is this?" The answer is not to be found in an intellectual analysis but always in the physical experience of the moment itself. There are no words that can ever capture the "whatness" of the visceral experience of the present moment. Yet in experiencing its unique and ever-changing texture in a non-conceptual way, we can find a satisfaction not available in a life based mainly on getting, on doing, on fixing.

So the practice is to simply let life be. This is not passivity or pseudodetachment. We still need the discipline to stay present, to remain still. The discipline is to choose in each moment not to spin off, to choose to be precise in our labeling and in our self-observation. We can practice this way both on and off the meditation cushion. The open mind that's willing to look at whatever arises—that wants simply to know, to be with, to reside in the reality of the moment—is always accessible to us.

Struggling as we do when we try to change or get rid of an experience—whether in our sitting practice or in our life—is always optional. "Suffering" also is optional. This may be hard to accept, especially when we are addicted to our suffering. But we don't have to suffer our suffering! We can just observe it, experience it for what it is, and let it be.

For example, suppose we have physical pain or discomfort. Usually this pain will be followed by believed thoughts such as "What's going to happen to me?" or "I can't believe this is happening." As soon as we get hooked into believing these thoughts, our suffering begins. The physical experience of discomfort becomes layered with the emotional suffering. In fact, these believed thoughts usually intensify and solidify our physical discomfort. Instead, we can choose to observe and label our thoughts and then let our experience just be. What happens to the pain? Perhaps you can try this and see.

Several years ago during a long period of intense illness, I had to have a blood test weekly. From my own early conditioning, I had developed a strong aversion to blood tests. Often I'd get dizzy, and sometimes I would even faint. My aversion wasn't rooted in fear of pain; it was simply a particular by-product of my conditioning. The fact that I saw this clearly didn't matter. I'd still show up for the tests with lots of anxiety. In coping I tried all the Zen practices I had learned through the years. For example, I'd go in for the blood test and focus totally on my breath. But I'd still faint. I'd say little mantras about spaciousness or about sitting there like a mountain, but it made no difference. Practicing like this to counteract what I perceived as weakness in myself may even have made things worse. In judging myself as "weak," I gave my conditioned reaction even more power.

But one day while driving to the lab, I remembered the practice I had recently learned: to ask "What *is* this?" to whatever presents itself. From the moment I sat in the chair to have my blood drawn, I kept this practice question before me, intent on experiencing the texture of the moment. When the dizziness began, instead of the anxiety and dread of aversion, I actually felt the excitement of curiosity. I was going to discover what fainting really feels like! However, I didn't faint. The dizziness passed, and I sat there quite at ease. When I gave up the struggle, not only did the unnecessary suffering disappear, but the physical experience transformed as well. Remember, I wasn't doing this practice in order to avoid the unpleasantness of fainting, which is how we often skew practice. That's what I had been doing before. In this case the willingness to just be with my experience disconnected the circuitry of my conditioning.

I'm not talking about calling our conditioning an empty illusion and pretending to let it go. That wouldn't be real. What I'm talking about is a certain lightness of heart that we can bring to our experience. Without our attempts to be spacious, spaciousness arises. It arises when we stop believing our judgments, especially the hard-hearted ones we make of ourselves. When we stop resisting what is and over time learn the willingness to be with it, we may even come to enjoy our repeating patterns, our little human drama, the whole passing show.

When we feel anxious, the practice is to hear the thoughts, feel the anxiety, and just let it be. When we feel tired or sleepy, the practice is to physically feel the sleepiness and then let it be. When we feel ourselves resisting the present moment, the practice is to truly feel the texture of that resistance and then simply let it be there.

Living from the open heart doesn't require getting rid of our fears, our unwanted feelings and personality traits, our difficult situations. The only things we have to give up are our opinions and self-judgments. Everything follows from that, especially the courage to be as we are, however we are. Being who we are, though, is not a license to do whatever we please under the guise of "spiritual freedom." It's about being willing to experience within ourselves whatever arises, without *needing* to make it different. When we see our drama and difficulties not as a catastrophe but just as conditioning, we can approach them with less heaviness and more compassion. As we experience our drama within this bigger container of awareness, we can begin to relax into our sitting and relax into our life.

Perhaps we will even get a glimpse of the profound yet simple truth that all we really need to learn is the willingness to be. We don't have to do or fix or change anything. In fact, as we enter deeply into the willingness to just be, we discover an abiding trust that seems to support us as we are. In our surrender to the moment, we experience the equanimity of the genuine life, free from the filter of our judgments or the need for anything to be different.

This surrender to the moment is the essence of living the practice life. Although it is so simple, it is also difficult to do consistently. Why? Because we're not willing. We don't want to be with life as it is. We want to believe our thoughts. But the practice life has to include seeing and working with this resistance—all the endless ways we obstruct our openness. And then we learn to come back, to simply be present, as best we can, with whatever our life is in this moment.

15

Loving-Kindness

A YEAR OR SO AFTER I BEGAN WORKING as a hospice volunteer, I was asked to sit with the body of a thirty-year-old man who had just died. He had requested that his body remain untouched for three days. He had specific beliefs about what happened following death, and his wish was for supportive people to sit with him through the process. Although I didn't know him, I agreed to sit with him for three hours the next morning.

Upon opening the door to his room and seeing the emaciated corpse on the bed, I immediately turned away. This young man had died of AIDS; and at the sight of his skin-and-bones corpse, I felt the fear of death. I spent the next few minutes distracting myself—lighting incense, looking at the many pictures of him on the wall—doing whatever I could not to look at him in the present moment. Then I remembered that I was there not for my own comfort but to honor his request for support. I walked over to the bed, stood next to him, and examined his body. It was still difficult for me to look at him. I knew that my discomfort was a direct reflection of my own fear of dying a painful death.

I made a sitting place on the bed next to his, and for the next three hours, I sat cross-legged, mostly doing a loving-kindness meditation toward his body. I don't want to romanticize this, because there were moments when I would drift off into daydreams or look at the body beside me and see only the corpse of someone with whom I had no connection. But as time passed, I gradually stopped seeing just an emaciated corpse and instead started connecting with this human being.

I would breathe the image of him into my heartspace on the inbreath, and on the outbreath I would silently say to him a version of the words of the loving-kindness meditation:

> May you dwell in the open heart.
> May you be free of your suffering.
> May you be healed in this moment, just as it is.
> May the awakened heart be extended to all beings.

At first these were just words. I had no feeling of loving-kindness to extend to him. In fact, I had only discomfort and fear. But the practice of loving-kindness is not about trying to feel some special way. It's about working with whatever is present, whatever blocks our natural kindness. So I stayed with my own discomfort, experiencing the physical reality of my emotional pain as I silently repeated the words of loving-kindness. Breathing into the heartspace, I began breathing in my own pain along with the image of the stranger next to me. Gradually the barriers between us, which were made of my own fear and defenses, began to break down.

As these barriers between us broke down, I was no longer experiencing his pain (as I perceived it) as separate from mine. In fact, what I felt was more like the universal pain that all human beings share. As I repeated the words of loving-kindness, a sense of deep connection began to replace my fear and discomfort. No longer was this just a stranger's body lying on the bed next to me. For brief moments the apparent barriers between us broke down, and I experienced a sense of the universal heart—the heart that is the essence of who we are, beyond separateness.

When I was in my early twenties, I came across the following lines from Thomas Wolfe: "Which of us has known his brother? . . . Which of us is not forever a stranger and alone?" At the time those words struck me to the core, but I didn't know the way out of my prison. Now, more than thirty years later, I can see what is required. Doing a loving-kindness practice is not a simple feel-good endeavor. It demands hard work. First we have to open ourselves to uncharted territory, beyond our normal agendas and protections. Then we must allow ourselves to see through the encrusted layers of fear and self-judgment that prevent real loving-kindness from coming forth. The problem, of course, is that for the most part we don't want to drop our agendas and protections.

Unfortunately the practice of loving-kindness is often presented in a way that bypasses dealing with our fears and self-judgments. It is easy to misuse this practice by trying to generate a loving feeling to cover over unhealed pain or by trying to seem more "loving." So what does it mean to awaken loving-kindness?

We could define loving-kindness as a sense of goodwill, a benign awareness, often accompanied by sensations of warmth and receptivity. This openness, this sense of allowing, diminishes the mind's tendency to constantly judge. Breathing into the heartspace somehow undercuts the solidity of our judgmental mind and allows us to access this capacity to be open, by which we can let ourselves, let others, let life, just be.

The practice itself is described in detail in the following chapter. On the inbreath we bring awareness, via the breath, into the center of the chest. Then on the outbreath we extend awareness from the heartspace toward ourselves or others. However, it is important to remember that in doing a practice like this, we are not trying to feel some special way, such as loving or kind. Rather, we are attending to how we are right now, which includes attending to whatever keeps our natural loving-kindness from streaming forth. At its most profound, the heart of loving-kindness is who we are. It is the nature of our being. Experiencing this often means first experiencing whatever gets in the way, especially our unloving behavior, unkind thoughts, and judgments about ourselves and others.

Sometimes it may be that we in fact do feel some sense of loving-kindness as we breathe into the heartspace. Just as often we may contact the anger and fear that are usually underneath our unkindness. Acknowledging and experiencing the anger and fear will allow our natural kindness to gradually begin to flow.

We can also access and cultivate loving-kindness directly. The "Way of the Pilgrim" is the story of a simple pilgrim who walked across the plains of nineteenth-century Russia. He carried only dried bread and two books—the Bible and an early Orthodox Christian text, the *Philokalia*—to sustain his body and his practice. With a genuine homesickness for God, his only aim was to learn how to pray without ceasing.

Although we're unlikely to ever be pilgrims in the old-fashioned sense, there is something real in the phrase "pray without ceasing." What is real is the same quality that makes a genuine loving-kindness practice so powerful. Real prayer is a genuine surrender to the moment, whatever the moment may be. It's not like the prayer of children, in the sense that we're asking that our wishes be granted. Real prayer is a deep opening to life itself, a deep listening, a willingness to just be with the moment. In this sense it is essentially no different from the practice of opening into the heart. When we do the loving-kindness meditation, we're not asking for something. Rather, by entering into the spaciousness of the heart, we're allowing life to just be.

What most gets in the way of this deep form of prayer is just what the pilgrim experienced: the constant desire to spin off into the comfort and security of thinking—into our plans, fantasies, dramas, and especially our believed judgments.

How do we counteract this very human tendency? Just like the pilgrim, we bring awareness to the breath, the heart, and the words of loving-kindness over and over. This is not easy. The pilgrim started with thirty minutes of prayer a day. Then his teacher told him to recite the prayer two thousand times a day. Then six thousand. Then twelve thousand. After years of practice, with wholehearted devotion and perseverance, the prayer became self-activating, and he could pray without ceasing. He experienced the delight of the heart bubbling over and a gratitude toward all things. He came to understand the meaning of the words "The kingdom of God is within." This example can give us the inspiration to bring a little more determination to our practice, allowing us to enter more regularly and deeply into the actual practice of loving-kindness.

As we practice loving-kindness on a regular basis, it is no longer just a meditation exercise. It becomes a part of our being, our natural response to life. We discover that when fear arises, we can see it, experience it, and learn to send nonjudgmental awareness into this fearful being. When illness arises, instead of seeing ourselves as defective or analyzing how we are ill because of this or that, we can just breathe into the heart, experiencing the whatness of who we are in that moment. We then extend loving-kindness into our physical body. This practice teaches us that we can receive even the most unwanted aspects of ourselves with a certain sense of spaciousness, warmth, and receptivity—which are the essence of loving-kindness.

As we learn to approach our "stuff" with less judgment, we'll begin to lose the tendency to use it against ourselves—as evidence that we're broken. When we cease our merciless judging, we experience the tenderness and warmth we are often unable to access out of fear of being unprotected, or out of the fear of deceiving ourselves. This is how we awaken our innate capacity for loving-kindness. Awakening loving-kindness means looking at our stuff, seeing it for what it is, greeting it with openness, meeting it without judgment, and then moving toward true healing, which is openly experiencing our natural wholeness.

16

Loving-Kindness Meditation

I CONSIDER THE MEDITATION EXERCISE in this chapter to be one of the single most important practices I've ever encountered. It is not meant to replace daily sitting but rather to complement it. I practice the meditation regularly, at a separate time from my daily sitting.

If you already do a loving-kindness meditation, it might be helpful to forget about it while you read and try this meditation, so that you can be open to whatever may be of value here.

The meditation consists of four-line rounds that repeat several times. The first round is oriented toward yourself; the second and following rounds are offered toward people close to you. The last round of the meditation is offered toward all beings.

First Round: Toward Yourself

Take a couple of deep breaths. Become aware of the breath and begin to follow it into the center of the chest. Experience the area around the heart. Does it feel closed and constricted? Does it feel clear and open? Does it feel warm or cool? Is it neutral? Whatever you feel, just be aware of that. With each inbreath let awareness go a little deeper.

Now begin to repeat the following four lines in rhythm with your breathing:

1. On the inbreath bring awareness, via the breath, into the center of the chest. As you exhale, silently say the words

> May I dwell in the open heart,

allowing whatever warmth may be present in the heart region to extend through your whole body, your whole being. If there is no warmth, no loving-kindness to extend, simply notice this and continue. Repeat the first line for several breaths.

2. On the inbreath again bring awareness into the heart region. As you exhale, say the words

> May I attend to whatever clouds the heart,

becoming aware of any aspect of yourself—anger, protections, self-judgment, basic fears—that blocks access to the open heart. Extend the warmth and loving-kindness of awareness into these aspects of yourself wherever you can feel them. Do this for a few breaths, remembering that you are not trying to get rid of anything. Rather, you are extending the compassion of awareness to these closed-off areas.

3. Continue breathing into the heart region. On the exhale say the third line:

> May I be awake in this moment, just as it is,

becoming aware of everything around you and within you—sounds, smells, sights, physical sensations, mood, thoughts—and letting yourself experience all of it, letting life be just as it is. Stay with this wide-open awareness for several breaths, continuing to breathe in and out of the heartspace. When the mind wanders, come back to your awareness of breath and heart softly, without self-judgment.

4. Again, breathe into the heartspace. On the outbreath say the words

May the awakened heart be extended to all beings,

extending whatever loving-kindness arises to other beings, including any specific people who may come into your awareness. Say this fourth line for several breaths.

Repeat this round of four lines again while breathing in and out of the heartspace:

May I dwell in the open heart.
May I attend to whatever clouds the heart.
May I be awake in this moment, just as it is.
May the awakened heart be extended to all beings.

Repeat this round of practice one more time.

Second Round: Toward a Loved One

Now bring into awareness the presence of someone close to you, for whom you have positive feelings, to whom you wish to extend loving-kindness.

Breathe the person's image, her presence, into the heartspace on the inbreath. On the outbreath extend loving-kindness toward this person while repeating the following four lines. If you feel resistance, just acknowledge and experience whatever is in the way.

May you dwell in the open heart.
May your suffering be healed.
May you be awake in this moment, just as it is.
May the awakened heart be extended to all beings.

More Rounds: Toward Others Close to You

Choose another person for whom you have positive feelings and repeat the four lines, remembering to breathe in and out of the heartspace as you say the words of loving-kindness.

Bring as many different people into your awareness as you wish, repeating the same process for each one.

Last Round: Toward All Beings

Finally expand awareness to all beings, however you conceive of this notion. Bring this awareness into the heartspace with the inbreath and with the outbreath repeat the following four lines, allowing loving-kindness to be extended to all beings:

> May the hearts of all beings be awakened.
> May the suffering of all beings be healed.
> May all beings be awake in this moment, just as it is.
> May all beings awaken their hearts to one another.

After completing all four rounds, come back to simply breathing in and out of the heartspace, experiencing the texture and quality of the heart. Simply experience whatever is there, going deeper with each inbreath.

Notes on the Loving-Kindness Meditation

The key to learning the power of this practice is to do it regularly. It is also helpful on occasion to do it repeatedly for a longer period of time, such as a whole day at a retreat.

The lines themselves are important in that they help us to focus and direct our attention. As with any other meditation, we will keep wandering off into daydreams, plans, and fantasies. In staying with the lines as best we can, we'll at the very least sharpen our focus.

These four lines correspond to the four basic stages of practice. The first line, "May I dwell in the open heart," corresponds to the initial stage in practice: the awakening of aspiration. The second line, "May I attend to whatever clouds the heart," corresponds to the long and difficult stage of working with all our protections, fears, and judgments. The third line, "May I be awake in this moment, just as it is," corresponds to the stage of wide-open awareness, in which we settle into being with life as it is. The last line, "May the awakened heart be extended to all beings,″ corresponds to the stage of moving from a self-centered view to a more life-centered view. Understanding the four lines in this way allows us to use them to continuously connect to the bigger picture of practice.

When I first started doing this meditation, using the words from a version I had learned, I described it to Joko. She questioned whether I was trying to feel some special way. I later realized that I was, in fact, trying to create a special state of mind. So I revised the wording to bring it into alignment with my overall understanding of practice, which is more about being with life as it is rather than trying to feel some special way. You, too, can experiment with changing the words to suit your own understanding.

Students often ask how these lines differ from affirmations. The answer goes to the very essence of the practice of loving-kindness. Affirmations are like mental injections we use to change or cover over our feelings. This practice is the opposite: it is not about changing or covering over our feelings; it is about experiencing whatever is present. Anyway, loving-kindness is not a feeling; it is the state of our being. What makes the loving-kindness practice more than a shallow mental exercise is the focus on the physical awareness of the heartspace. We experience all the images, all the lines, through the awareness of the breath in and out of the heartspace. This focus on breathing in and out of the heart takes the loving-kindness meditation beyond the mental realm.

How do we choose those to whom we extend loving-kindness? Some practitioners, in order to work with their negative feelings, choose people with whom they are experiencing difficulty. This is tricky. It's possible to use the meditation to fool ourselves into thinking that we are free from negativity when, in fact, we've just covered it over. I usually work directly with strong negative feelings toward another person away from the loving-kindness meditation. I reserve the loving-kindness meditation for those for whom I currently have a positive regard.

But this is certainly an area worthy of personal experiment.

I bring the same people into this meditation every time I do it. Occasionally, when someone I know is ill or in distress, I will include him as well. I also include a few friends who are no longer alive, using each to represent one of my own fears. For example, two people I am currently practicing with are former hospice patients. One had a great fear of losing control; the other had a strong fear of physical pain. I bring them in for just one breath with the line "May you dwell in the open heart," extending loving-kindness toward them in their fear. I then follow with one breath toward myself and my own similar fears. In doing this, I've learned to bring a sense of heart and spaciousness to fears that before seemed unworkable.

At first it may feel uncomfortable to experience the breath in and out of the heartspace. It may also feel foreign to silently repeat the words of loving-kindness. It's worth the effort, however, to stay with your initial discomfort or cynicism. I know of no other practice so effective in undercutting the solidity of the judgmental mind or in helping break through our chronic state of separateness. The power of breathing in and out of the heartspace can't be explained or denied. The only way to feel it is to make this meditation an integral and regular part of your practice life.

Don't be surprised if doing this practice brings up doubt and resistance. We have a tendency to use practice as protection. The openness of this loving-kindness meditation can seem threatening. You may feel that you are deceiving yourself or that somehow the practice is not genuine. But even if you believe these conditioned judgments, it doesn't mean that they're true. The more you can suspend your judgmental mind, the more you can be open to what's of value.

17

Awakening the Heart of Compassion

WHEN I STARTED TO RECOVER from the first prolonged episode of my immune disorder, I felt strongly motivated to stay close to the edge. I'd learned so much from being acutely ill that I didn't want to fall back into a life routine based mostly on cultivating comfort and security. Having faced my fears related to dying, I wanted to keep the fact of death in front of me as a reminder not to go back to skating on thin ice. I knew how easy it would be to lose my deepened connection with the aspiration to awaken.

But I wasn't sure how, realistically, to keep myself close to the edge. Hoping for direction, I took a class in "Death and Dying." Although the class itself was of no substantial help, what came out of it was the opportunity to participate as a volunteer at the local hospice. Although I knew at once that I wanted to become a hospice volunteer, it was hard for me to imagine going into the home of a stranger dying of cancer, AIDS, or some other terminal disease. I would be going in as a volunteer to do what? Who was I to be in this situation? What was I to say? How could I possibly help a dying person in her suffering? In spite of my doubts, I took the training and began what was to become one of the most powerful learning paths I have ever encountered.

Be Open to Change

When I was assigned my first patient, Richard (whose name I have changed here, as I have with all the hospice patients and their families), a fifty-two-year-old with terminal brain cancer, I was still experiencing discomfort and self-doubt. I decided to get acquainted briefly with Richard a few days before making my first hospice visit. Although I made this unofficial visit on the pretext of making Richard feel more comfortable, in truth it was to make *me* feel more comfortable. His wife answered the door and took me to meet her husband, who was standing in a dark hallway. After speaking for a minute in a friendly way, Richard blurted out, "It's hopeless!" and walked into his room, closing the door. As I turned to his wife, she said, "I'm terrified," and started to cry. She quickly walked away from me, and not knowing what to do, I left the house. I was so stunned by what had happened that all I could do was sit in my car for a while.

When I got home, I called my hospice supervisor, who tried to reassure me. I meditated a lot over the next few days, trying to ground myself in the reality of the moment, but the anxiety and self-doubt remained. By the time I returned to Richard's, I was braced for the worst, with a variety of contingency plans. When his wife answered the door with a smile and took me in to see Richard, who was cheerfully watching wrestling on television, I was thrown almost as off balance as on the first visit. In both cases I had gone in with expectations—based entirely on mental pictures—of who to be and what to do.

That I needed to be open to change, to the unexpected, without the illusion that I could substantially control or change anything, is a lesson I learned over and over again, not just from patient to patient but from one visit to the next. Often conditions were changing so rapidly that they could never be pinned down with a formulaic response. This meant giving up the comfort of my familiar identities of who to be and what to do. Without dropping my identity as "the helper" and my mental picture of the patient as someone to be helped, I would never have been able to connect in a meaningful way. The challenge—and the opportunity—was to report for each hospice visit without expecting results or needing to fix the situation. Instead, it was just to offer my own being, my basic human kindness, even when there was no apparent personal connection with the other person. To participate fully was to be open without preconceptions to whatever presented itself.

During one visit Richard told me about the day he buried his father. As he was kneeling at his father's grave, he heard his father say, "If you wish to see me in heaven, you'd better straighten up your life." Only a year earlier, when his father had implored him to give up drinking and cursing, Richard had retorted angrily, "You live your life, and I'll live mine." But upon hearing the voice at the grave, he turned his life completely around. Not only did he give up drinking and cursing, he also began to pray every day. For the first time in his life, he felt a sense of equanimity. Although he didn't want to die, he now trusted God's plans and viewed death as a positive transition.

The experience at the grave had transformed Richard's life. Though from my own perspective he did not exude deep spiritual understanding, I could not deny that he seemed to regard his illness and approaching death with genuine acceptance. To expect him to follow my agenda for what a spiritual experience should look like would have been irrelevant and would also have prevented our experiencing a real connection. His heart was truly attuned to his own understanding of God, and there was nothing that I needed to do or say. I could just listen and feel the beauty of this gentle human being.

It became clear to me that often all the path of compassion requires us to "do" is give up our need to control situations and to change other people to fit our preconceived notions. As we learn to be open to whatever presents itself and to offer our own being in return, we experience the basic connectedness that is the heart of compassion.

Don't Hold Back Your Heart

Mary was a sixty-nine-year-old patient with heart disease and emphysema. She spent most of her time in bed, hooked up to a catheter and oxygen. In spite of her deteriorating condition, she was warm and friendly when I visited, though an underlying anxiety and agitation was undeniable. For example, she had to keep a video running or the television on twenty-four hours a day, and she was too restless to watch a movie or a show all the way through. Yet she was not interested in talking about her anxiety as much as she was in just trying to keep it at bay.

During my first visits, my only function seemed to be that of a glorified baby-sitter. But as I got to know Mary and see how difficult it was for her to cope with her fears, I began to feel for her. I practiced learning to speak to her from the heart, silently saying the words "May you dwell in the open heart. May your suffering be healed." Though I never imagined I was having a spiritual communication with her or that she was even receiving my words of loving-kindness, as I continued the practice of silently speaking from the heart, a sense of genuine connection with her began to deepen.

On one visit while we were watching a video, I felt the impulse to hold her hand. Then I hesitated, thinking it might make her feel uncomfortable. When I got home later, I felt sorry that I had held myself back. Resolving not to let my doubts and anxieties get in the way the next time, I began to look forward to holding her hand and to having a warm visit. But the day I was to see her again, I received a call that Mary had just died.

What affected me more than the sadness I felt was the realization that I would never again have the opportunity to make the simple gesture of touching her hand. I had given in to the doubts of my small mind, and by the time I had become aware of this, it was too late to express my open heart. The lesson was clear and powerful: time passes swiftly, and with it, our only chance. The words that were painfully etched into my being, and that subsequent hospice visits brought up time and time again, were: "Don't hold back your heart in fear."

Attend to Your Own Agendas

Maureen was only in her midforties, but by the time we met, the cancer in her liver had left her with only a few weeks to live. I was specifically assigned to Maureen because she had asked for a hospice worker who could talk to her about her spiritual practice. Upon sharing our experiences of both illness and meditation, we connected immediately. She seemed quite open to what I had to say, and she liked occasionally hearing the guided meditations I read to her from Stephen Levine's *Healing into Life and Death*. She was the first hospice patient to whom I spoke about how, very specifically, to work with her experience.

Much of our conversation revolved around Maureen's disappointment with her family. She felt frustrated that her husband and teenage daughters seemed unable to accept that she was dying. They related to her as if she were well, with the cancer being seen as a temporary inconvenience. But her bigger problem was with herself. A compliant person, she was driven to try to live up to their picture of her as essentially healthy. She would not ask for help for fear of disrupting their image-based world. I tried to help her see that living out of false pictures—both her family's and her own—was causing her distress and disappointment as well as preventing any genuine connection with those she loved.

But Maureen's sense of isolation and separateness increased as her body deteriorated. One day hospice called to say that she had suffered a major downturn and was probably near death. When I went to see her, she was too sick for more than a very brief visit. The pained and frightened look on her face sharpened the frustration I felt at not being able to help her.

Driving home, I felt the frustration change into a more

intense distress, complete with sensations of nausea and heaviness. When I arrived, I had a strong impulse to get busy, to avoid being with the discomfort. But knowing that my emotional reaction was a sign of something I wasn't seeing, I sat down to meditate instead. I tried to stay with the physical feeling of distress, asking myself "What *is* this?" I was not seeking a logical or conceptual answer but rather an experiential one. I was nauseous, and my body was tight all over, suffused with vague feelings of gloom, defeat, and rejection.

It gradually became clear that my distress was a direct (and predictable) consequence of my own unrecognized agendas. I had seen myself as a person who could help, the hospice saint who would help ease Maureen's pain and guide her to a "conscious death." Of course, this was not my only motivation. But it was obvious to me that my hidden agendas had been getting in the way of any genuine connection. My need to help had prevented me from seeing that there was little I could have done to help reverse her or her family's deep-seated patterns. As all this became clear, the feelings of distress dissipated. I then turned my mind to Maureen, remembering her pained, confused, and frightened face. I began breathing her presence into the heartspace, extending to her loving-kindness. My need to help, and even more so my need to be appreciated, had prevented me from making this genuine offering.

Although she died within hours of our last visit, I still remember Maureen regularly even today. I often breathe her presence into my heartspace, feeling the pain of living from fear-based agendas: hers of not being able to address her pattern of conforming to an image of who she was supposed to be, and mine of needing to be appreciated as someone who helped. In experiencing these all-too-human tendencies within the spaciousness of the heart, the warmth of loving-kindness replaces the heaviness of distress.

The natural impulse to help, to give, to connect, will often be enmeshed with more self-centered agendas—wanting to be seen as a helper, wanting to achieve results from doing, needing to be appreciated. These smaller agendas will often impede the natural urge to act in a compassionate way. Only by seeing through them over and over, as well as by experiencing the havoc that they wreak, can we loosen their power to pollute our natural compassion.

Death Is a Closed Heart

Thomas was a sixty-nine-year-old Irishman dying of liver and pancreatic cancer. Even though we had little in common on the surface, we nonetheless connected from our first visit. As I found out later, people who are close to death often feel the need to tell their story. They don't want us to reinterpret their difficult situation in a more positive way—they just want to be heard. With Thomas, it was apparent right away that this was what he wanted from our encounters; for me, it was equally important to learn how to just listen, beyond my normal agendas and identities. I would ask him a few questions and then simply let him tell his story, in his thick brogue. I didn't comment on his story, nor try to make him feel better about his "mistakes," nor let him pull me into its melodramatic aspects. Instead, I simply listened, as much as I was able.

Over the next few weeks, I got to know Thomas well and gradually became very fond of him. He had a lot of pride, particularly around his independence. For example, one of his daughters had crossed him at some point to go her own way, and he couldn't forgive her in spite of the obvious pain that their separation caused him. Also, he could not allow himself to need others or to be taken care of; he had to see himself as not having needs. One day, after he had been in the bathroom for fifteen minutes, I knocked on the door to see whether he was OK. He said he was fine, but after a few more minutes, I knocked again and opened the door. He was standing in front of the mirror trying to button the snap on his pajama bottoms to the buttonhole on his pajama top. Although he was totally confused and helpless, he couldn't ask for help. He couldn't move beyond his deeply embedded pride of independence.

As his body deteriorated and he became more dependent, I watched Thomas struggle with the fear of helplessness. With sadness I also watched how even in his last days, he couldn't let his daughter back into his heart. I knew from my own life that suffering in itself is not the key to transformation. Only when we are willing to learn from our suffering can transformation occur. Unwilling to surrender, Thomas died as he had lived.

I have never talked directly to a hospice patient about my own views on "death and dying." In fact, I have tried to resist adopting a firm position about what death is, because in truth, I don't know. What has become increasingly clear to me from my own struggles, both physical and emotional, is that we are much more than our bodies, our thoughts, our identities. Who we really are is life's energy flowing through us. To open our heart means experiencing this river of love that we are and allowing it to manifest as and through our conditioned package. This is our true healing. Rather than concerning ourselves with what happens after the death of the body, we can attend to and heal the "deaths within life." These are the deaths we feel each time the heart is closed—in anger, in fear, in protective stances and strategies, in avoiding pain, in resisting the unpleasant. Thomas was a vivid and sad reminder to me that by maintaining our protections, we encase ourselves in a substitute life. As long as we maintain our pride of independence or our fear of the unknown or our need to control, we can never become awake to our genuine life—which is Life itself, unfettered with the notion of "self."

Like a White Bird in the Snow

Larry was a forty-eight-year-old artist and teacher who was diagnosed with lung cancer. He'd been told that he had about six months to live. A quiet and thoughtful man, his basic out-look when I met him was "What's the use?" He had not com-pletely given up, however, and was willing to engage with me in genuine conversation. Perhaps his strongest emotion was the sadness and grief he felt over the prospect of not being able to see his teenage sons grow up.

As weeks passed and my rapport with Larry grew stronger, I felt an increasing sense of agitation whenever I was with him. His believed thoughts of hopelessness were contributing to his suffering, and it was difficult for me to watch him sink further into a self-imposed isolation. I wanted to reach out to him, to grab him and shake him, to shout to him to wake up to the fact that he wasn't dead yet! He could still enjoy his children, his beautiful garden, the preciousness of being alive. But he wasn't asking for my help.

Although drawn by a longing to ease his suffering, I was also aware that my continued reactivity to Larry's situation was strong enough to warrant inspection. As I sat with my agitation and longing to help, it became increasingly clear why I felt such a strong need to "fix" him. Since I still needed him to be a par-ticular way, it was obvious that I wasn't coming from a place of real compassion but more from my own unhealed pain. His basic stance of hopelessness and withdrawal resembled one of my own historical responses to difficulty, and his particular brand of self-imposed suffering was one that I also had often experienced.

As I sat with the anxiety and sadness that Larry triggered in me and invited it into the spaciousness of the heart, it became clear to me how presumptuous it was to want to take away his pain. His pain contained the ripe possibility of surrendering to what is, just as did mine. Within our pain rests the grace that will often arise if we allow ourselves to surrender. Realizing our shared pain deepened my bond with Larry. I no longer need-ed him to experience a "meaningful death." I no longer needed to take away his suffering. Instead, as I would breathe my own pain into the heart, I would include his pain as well. At certain points our individual pain began to merge until it was no longer "my" pain or "his" pain, but the pain that we all share. This was not morbid or depressing; in fact, what I experienced was a depth of understanding and a profound sense of connection.

I realized that genuine compassion can never come from fear or from the longing to fix or change. Compassion results naturally from the realization of our shared pain. It manifests as we grow out of our own sense of separateness, isolation, and alienation. In my subsequent visits with Larry, my agitation changed into the wish to just be present with him.

One evening Larry had a massive hemorrhage and was taken to intensive care. At this same time, there were some difficult family dynamics that none of the participants seemed able to pull back from. Driving to the hospital, I knew that I might get involved in this very messy situation. I was also aware of my strong aversion to the hospital environment. But I was equally aware that Larry might be very close to death, and as I rode the elevator up to his room, I kept repeating to myself, almost as a mantra, "This may be the last time you see him alive. Don't hold back your heart."

The visit was difficult. Larry spoke frankly about dying as well as about his bitter feelings around the family dysfunction. I struggled to stay open, to avoid falling back into familiar patterns of self-protection. I also chose to speak to two family members after Larry made it clear to me that he wasn't capable of dealing with the family scene. Afterward, as I sat in my car in the hospital parking lot, I couldn't stop the tears. In part I was seeing how much pain we inflict on one another out of self-protection. In part I was feeling how intact the shell of protection around my own heart was. But mostly the tears came from feeling that shell cracking open, with love flowing out, ready to be offered. This was a taste of my true aspiration: to learn to live from the open heart, to give—not from "should," not from "in order to," not "for" anything—simply because it is the natural order of the unobstructed heart to give, like a white bird in the snow.

Larry died at home a few days later. During his last few hours, I faced him as he lay in bed. Although he appeared to be in a coma, he had one eye wide open. For one incredible half hour, I sat gazing into his eye, which seemed to be looking intently right back at me. Looking at his emaciated body and catching glimpses of the word LOVE hanging from a mobile above his head reminded me again and again to stay out of protection and just offer my own being. Who is to say what actually transpired? I sensed that our connection served to anchor him as he approached his death. He died half an hour after I left.

The Open Heart Knows Only Connection

James was seventy-six years old when we met, dying from lung cancer and heart failure and confined mostly to lying in bed. Although he was very weak, he would always try to be friendly and pleasant. He would even force himself to stay awake so that he would not appear to be rude. Although I was fond of him, our contact wasn't deep, nor did I feel I was serving him in any significant way.

After my first few visits, he started to decline rapidly, particularly with the onset of intermittent dementia. He often didn't know who or where he was. Frequently he would look at me and just smile, laughing almost silently to himself like a baby. I felt joy in his sweetness and in his appreciation of the moment. He would also lie for long periods without speaking. Then I would sit by him and do the loving-kindness meditation, relating to him from the heart but not with spoken words. Relating to him silently from the heart, I was no longer relating to him as a psychological persona or as an emaciating physical package. The relationship was more being-to-being. Experiencing him in this way, I felt less and less uncomfortable about his declining physical condition. In fact, as the sense of connection and intimacy grew, I found my time with James to be more and more fulfilling.

Gradually James fell into a coma, and I tried to visit him for a little while each day. I would sit by his bed holding his hand, breathing his presence into the heartspace, silently repeating the words of loving-kindness. Often I would feel the impulse to hold back. Out of self-consciousness or self-doubt or protectedness, I would want to retreat into the false comfort of familiar patterns. But part of the loving-kindness practice is to attend to whatever clouds the open heart, whatever solidifies the sense of separateness. When fear would arise, or the pain of holding back, I would experience their sensations within the spaciousness of the heart. As fear would subside, the sense of warmth and loving-kindness would again naturally flow. When the self-imposed prison walls come down, all that remains is the connectedness that we are.

As it became apparent that James was nearing death, I visited him to say good-bye. After sitting with him for a while, even though he was apparently in a deep coma, I spoke to him out loud from what was in my heart. Then, as I held his hand, I leaned over and whispered to him that this might be "good-bye." As I kissed his forehead, he squeezed my hand with unmistakable strength. In that moment I experienced the profound sense of connection that is the nature of our being. The sense of boundlessness and love was unfettered, and although it did not take long for me to erect the walls again, it became clear that this little mind cannot even begin to imagine the magnitude of the spaciousness of the heart.

What Is Our Life About?

OUR ASPIRATION, OUR CALLING, our desire for a
   genuine life,
is to see the truth of who we really are—
that the nature of our Being is connectedness and love,
not the illusion of a separate self to which our suffering
   clings.
It is from this awareness that Life can flow through us;
the Unconditioned manifesting freely as our conditioned
   body.

And what is the path?
To learn to reside in whatever life presents.
To learn to attend to all those things
that block the flow of a more open life;
and to see them as the very path to awakening—
all the constructs, the identities,
the holding back, the protections,
all the fears, the self-judgments, the blame—
all that separates us from letting life be.

And what is the path?
To turn away from constantly seeking comfort
and from trying to avoid pain.
To open to the willingness to just be,
in this very moment,
exactly as it is.

No longer so ready to be caught
in the relentlessly spinning mind.
Practice is about awakening to the true Self:
no one special to be,
nowhere to go,
just Being.

We are so much more than just this body,
just this personal drama.
As we cling to our fear,
and our shame, and our suffering,
we forsake the gratitude of living from our natural being.

So where, *in this very moment*, do we cling to our views?

Softening around the mind's incessant judgment,
we can awaken the heart that seeks to be awakened.

And when the veil of separation rises,
Life simply unfolds as it will.
No longer caught in the self-centered dream,
we can give ourselves to others,
like a white bird in the snow.

Time is fleeting.
Don't hold back.
Appreciate this precious life.

I wrote "What Is Our Life About?" the day before my fiftieth birthday. My intention was to read it daily in order to help rekindle my aspiration and to remind me of what is important. Since then I have revised it slightly to reflect subtle changes in my understanding of practice. It is now read as part of service at Zen centers, and many have found it helpful in clarifying the practice path.